UNEMPLOYED, But Moving On!

Smart Job Searching in a Web-Based World and a Sucky Economy

UNEMPLOYED
But Moving On!
Smart Job Searching in a Web-Based World and a Sucky Economy

Cheryl Butler Long

Impact Publications
Manassas Park, VA

Unemployed, But Moving On

ISBN: 978-1-57023-325-8 (13-digit); 1-57023-325-8 (10-digit)

Library of Congress: 2011933624

Publisher: For information on Impact Publications, including current and forthcoming publications, authors, press kits, online bookstore, and submission requirements, visit the left navigation bar on the front page of the publisher's main company website: www.impactpublications.com.

Publicity/Rights: For information on publicity, author interviews, and subsidiary rights, contact the Media Relations Department: Tel. 703-361-7300, Fax 703-335-9486, or email: query@impactpublications.com.

Sales/Distribution: All bookstore sales are handled through Impact's trade distributor: National Book Network, 15200 NBN Way, Blue Ridge Summit, PA 17214, Tel. 1-800-462-6420. All special sales and distribution inquiries should be directed to the publisher: Sales Department, IMPACT PUBLICATIONS, 9104 Manassas Drive, Suite N, Manassas Park, VA 20111-5211, Tel. 703-361-7300, Fax 703-335-9486, or email: query@impactpublications.com.

CONTENTS

DEDICATION

This book is dedicated to my husband, John Long,
who has always been there to support and believe in me,
and who always tries to convince me that even my lamest
ideas are the greatest things he's ever heard.

Introduction

Welcome to the Rough and Tough New Job Economy

You don't have to tell me how rough it is out there. I'm immersed, head and shoulders, in the misery of this job market and this sucky economy. I work every single day with people just like you, people who, usually through no fault of their own, are out of work, the victims of a government that has rewarded corporations for sending your jobs overseas or south of the border and an economy run by a cabal of Wall Street power brokers, intent on best serving their high-class clients and big business. The middle class be damned.

You're out of work and you're probably scared. Outwardly, you try to "man-up" (or "woman-up," as the case may be) and keep a positive attitude. But you've probably been out of work for some time now, haven't you? Still, you say, something's gotta give, you'll bounce back. Wrong. If you just sit back and wait for the economy to change and the perfect job to land in your lap as if by magic, you'll be on food stamps this time next year, assuming you're not already.

...
It's going to take work to find work.
...

You're going to have to **change your approach** to the problem, along with the way you're conducting your job search. It's going to take work to find work. You're going to have to **do research**. You're going to have to take a hard look at the

1

kind of work you can do in this new economy, and you may have to **make some tough career decisions**.

I can't promise you a job, but this book can help. Why should you read it? Why not? What else is working for you right now?

If you actually have a job at the present time and you're reading this out of curiosity, I have this to say to you: Go do the job they're paying you for. If you have a job, hang on to it; buy into the idea that you need this job, and do it with passion and commitment, giving them their money's worth. Because, trust me on this, you're most likely not going to find another one right now, and your employer can find a hundred candidates to take your place in the next 30 minutes if they so desire. If you don't have a job and you need one, read this book with an open mind. I sugarcoat nothing. I'm telling you what you need to know. It might not be easy to hear, but it's the current truth about people working or finding work in a sucky economy.

> ...
> **If you have a job, hang on to it; and do it with passion and commitment.**
> ...

Okay, you're asking yourself, "Why should I listen to this (insert your noun here)? Isn't she just getting paid to tell us all this b.s.?" The answer is: No, it's not about money. I'm writing this because I've spent the last seven years trying to help people find jobs who weren't (1) in any way prepared to search for a job, (2) qualified to land the jobs they were interested in, or (3) being told the real truth about why they would never get the job they actually wanted.

I'm a Workforce Development Specialist for a mid-western state. I'm supposed to show people how to write resumes that nobody will ultimately see. These resumes are the same as the last thousand resumes the Human Resources representative has seen because everybody knows the traditional resume uses the outdated "reverse-chronological" format. Well, not anymore, Jack!

I'm supposed to coach job seekers in the old-fashioned way to approach interviews because everybody knows you're supposed to wear the standard black or navy blue business "uniform" and answer the questions in exactly the way they've always been answered. That's assuming you even get to the interview stage. Whatever you do, you must exhibit the corporate look and display the corporate behavior.

I'm not supposed to notice that my clients are wearing nose rings and their pants expose at least six inches of underwear and that the actual waistband of those pants hits somewhere around their knees. More importantly, I'm just not supposed to comment on it, or mention the fact that the only job they'll ever get looking like that is in distribution for the local crack manufacturer.

I'm supposed to have a positive attitude and assure everyone that if they get additional training to upgrade their skills and follow all of the tips my agency gives out in its workshops and on its website, they will become gainfully employed and live happily ever after. Get a grip. It just isn't that easy anymore.

This book is based on my training, knowledge, and experience in the workforce development field. It's not so much based on the projections of "experts," because right now, as volatile as the U.S. job market has proven to be, I don't believe there really are experts. Nobody since the 1930s has seen a time quite as hard on job seekers. The people who refer to our economy as being in a "recession" have a particular agenda: not panicking the public. The reality is, economic and jobs statistics don't bear out the conservative label of "recession." If you look at all of the people on welfare of one variety or another, at the necessary proliferation of social service organizations and the speed with which those organizations use up their funds or other assistance sources, and the general tone of politics and fear in not only our country, but worldwide, there can be only one label: "Depression." Or, as I refer to it, "Depression 2: The Unofficial Sequel."

> ...
> **Nobody since the 1930s has seen a time quite as hard on job seekers. Economic and jobs statistics don't bear out the conservative label of "recession."**
> ...

Am I an economic expert? NO! Do I see what's going on on a daily basis? Absolutely, YES! I get my nose rubbed in it every single day when I deal with people who haven't worked in one, two, three years or more. The work just isn't there. Where is it? Mexico. India. Anywhere but these United States. I have to point them in the right direction to become employed again and give them hope. I just wish somebody would show me the signpost that indicates that direction and tell me what facts we should all base that hope upon. I could certainly use that information to pass on to my clients, who are hurting.

So, am I qualified to rule on whether or not we are having a Depression? Probably not. But, as the old saying goes, "If it looks like a duck, walks like a duck, and quacks like a duck, it's probably a duck." When I look at our jobless rate, or the homeless camps, I see a duck.

Is this book based on hard statistics and quotable sound bites from government or economic analysts? No. As I said, it's based on my training, knowledge, and experience in the field, and much of it reflects my seasoned opinion. You also know what they say about opinions: "They're like a-holes. Everybody's got one." Well, I've certainly got my opinions and I'll be happy to share them with you. You're welcome.

1
The Way We Were

Five Job Search Strategies and Assumptions That Have Bit the Dust

Things have changed, for sure. Music, styles, family structures, food, politics, economics. It would be easier to ask, "What, in our world, hasn't changed radically in the last, oh, five or ten years?" Let's take a look at a few preconceptions that have gone the way of the rainforests, cheap Las Vegas buffets, and knowing for sure that Social Security will be waiting for you at 60-something.

1. My high school diploma will get me a job.

Are you serious? If you believe this, I'm guessing that you're at least 50 years old. That's because those of us born before, say 1965, were pretty much led to believe that all we really needed was a high school diploma. College was the territory of rich kids or those who were looking for a way to keep from going into the military and getting sent to Vietnam. Guys graduated from high school, maybe went to a vocational/technical school, got a job, got married and started a family. Or they jumped the gun by choosing a branch of the military or a specialty within the service that would ensure them of not having to go to Nam. Some went to Canada.

Girls didn't have as many vocational options in that era. I remember being told by my parents that they couldn't afford to send me to college, so I could get married or become a secretary, period. I learned to type and take shorthand like a fiend because I didn't have any marital candidates lined up and my parents were already planning to move to an apartment that didn't include a room for me. Type or starve.

2. My college degree will get me a job.

When, as a married, working adult, I finally started college, I toyed with majors and career directions. I spoke with professionals who told me it didn't matter what discipline you got your degree in, companies only cared that you had one. My direct supervisor at the time—I was, of course, his secretary—told me that his degree was in History. He ran an enormous warehouse. Clearly, he must have been right about it not making a difference if your degree was in Fashion Merchandising because he had become successful in a field totally unrelated to his degree. You could still get a good job in Marketing or Product Development, couldn't you?

I started out intending to be a high school English teacher, then fell victim to the lure of big money. My faculty advisor told me that if I had a degree in Communications, I could land a job with IBM starting somewhere in the thirties and move up from there. Sounded good! At least it was better than having to put up with smart-ass teenagers every day. I looked long and hard at why I had wanted to be a teacher in the first place. I decided that, if the best thing I could say about my chosen career was that I wouldn't have to do it for three months in the summer each year, I was going into it for the wrong reasons.

Long story short, I graduated with two bachelor of arts degrees, one in Communication and one in Public Relations, and I quickly discovered that both of those degrees qualified me to sell used cars or manage fast food restaurants. I went on to get a master of liberal arts to complete the useless set. If I could just land a PhD, my employment horizons would be endless. Right.

In the years since my graduation, and based on my work in the workforce development field, I've discovered that just having a college degree isn't enough. It has to be the **right** college degree, and, in many cases, it has to be from the **right college**. If you want to get a job with a really noteworthy company—a Fortune 500 company, for instance—your junior college associate degree isn't going to cut it. The big companies want Ivy League degrees and they need to be relevant in today's job market. Can you say "Green Jobs"? Your degree needs to be somehow related to the new Green Economy or you'll be interviewing for those car sales or burger management jobs like the rest of us liberal arts majors.

> ...
> **Having a college degree isn't enough. It has to be the right college degree.**
> ...

Are you ready for another really rude awakening? Nobody cares what your grade point average was. Honestly. It just doesn't matter. If it was good enough, you graduated; if it wasn't, you didn't. If the certificate doesn't say Harvard…. Well, you get the idea.

3. My work experience will get me a job.

And a quarter will get you a cup of coffee. In what universe? Job experience isn't the be-all-and-end-all that it used to be. Oh, sure, you **need** some, but experience **alone** isn't going to cut it. You need a magical combination (diploma + degree + experience + connections + good luck) to get a job these days, and experience is only one component. It is, however, a component that you must have as **part** of the combination, but the key is also to not have **too much**.

I know, you're confused. Let me see if I can clarify a few things. As I've already said, a high school diploma or a non-Ivy League degree, by themselves, won't get you hired. Neither will having spent the last 20 years working for a single corporation or slaving away in a non-Green industry. The proof is all around us.

> •••
>
> **You need a magical combination (diploma + degree + experience + connections + good luck) to get a job these days.**
>
> •••

How many people do you know or you have heard of through your network, who have been employed most of their working lives for a single employer? They worked year after year after year, never missing a day because they were sick or their child needed both parents there when their tonsils were removed. They never took off when the car broke down; they just called a friend or took a bus or saddled up the family dog, whatever it took to show up on time. Somehow, they got their butts to work because that was their work ethic. They worked sick, tired, stressed out, and worried. They took on extra assignments when they were ready to drop, because the boss asked them to. They punched that time clock exactly on time, never late, and never left early. And after 20, 30, even 40 years, they retired. Do you know any of those people? There are fewer and fewer among us.

Clients who sit at my desk and tell me their stories share the following scenario. They were close to that 20- or 25- year retirement goal line. They were looking forward to those years and planning on that cabin at the lake or the RV they would use to travel the country or visit the grandkids in another state.

Then what happened is what you can probably guess happened. Their company was eyeing that goal line as well. They looked at Walter Worker and saw that in the next X number of months they were going to be saddled with that guy as a retiree for the rest of his natural life, and that was going to mean paying him his retirement salary and his health benefits and maybe even continued company perks or other benefits. They saw that the window for getting rid of this detriment was quickly closing, and they decided to start working on alleviating that problem.

Walter was going to start getting watched very closely and criticized for nitpicky things that everybody else working for the company was doing, too, and probably had been doing without repercussions for years. The difference is—and you can take this to your bookie and bet on it—Walter was going to get canned for something, anything, sometime between today and the day he would normally be receiving that gold watch. That is the way dedication is rewarded in today's corporate environment.

Get a little job experience in your field with as good a company as you can find. Spend a year, two, or three years there. Then move on. Don't put all of your career eggs in one corporate basket. And don't expect the same dedication from the company to their workforce that your company expects of you to the corporate flag. Loyalty, in employment, is seldom reciprocal these days.

4. My resume will get me a job.

I recently saw a resume that was supposed to be inspirational. It was called "The Resume of Jesus Christ." I know it makes me a sacrilegious pig, but I looked at that resume with the eye of a hiring manager and said to myself, "He couldn't get a job in today's economy." Granted, He definitely has a good personal Network and knows all the right People, but here we go again with relevant qualifications and experience. If I were a hiring manager, I would probably lean toward the "Over-qualified" label, if I needed to hire someone who would work cheap, do exactly what the supervisor asks them to do, and not rock the corporate boat in any way. Please don't grab your torches and pitchforks yet. I use this story to make a point.

> ...
> **The purpose
> of the resume is to
> get you an interview and
> to demonstrate
> what you can
> offer the company
> as a potential
> employee.**
> ...

The very best resume, with the best qualifications any person has ever had, will not get you hired. That's because getting you hired is not even the "responsibility" of the resume. The purpose of the resume is to get you an **interview**. It is designed to showcase your talents, knowledge, skills, experience, and education, to demonstrate what **you** can offer **the company** as a potential employee. Let me say that again. Its purpose is to demonstrate what you can offer the company. We're going to go into the fundamentals of resume construction and intent a little later, but, for now, just keep that in mind. The inspiring Resume of Jesus Christ wouldn't get Jesus the job and might not even get Him an interview. If He did land the interview, He would have to impress that corporate drone with His abilities and His desire to serve the corporate bottom line, and turning water into wine, although admirable, would probably not be seen as a marketable job skill. Go figure.

5. I can just change my employment field.

You're so cute when you're being naïve! I applaud your determination, your desire to move in a new direction, and I offer you this tidbit of advice: **Get real.** I'm not saying that to be mean, because I, myself, have done the very same thing. I started out as a secretary, moved to the world of law enforcement, then the corporate arena, and now I find myself in Workforce Development for state government. The difference is simple. I did it many, many years ago. Remember what I've been saying all along? "Things have changed." Let's chant that together: "Things have changed! Things have changed." Embroider that on a throw pillow.

Gone are the days when you could just decide that you were bored with being a fast food manager or a bus driver or a farmer. You could just start applying for jobs you had never held before until you found somebody who would take a chance on a person who was willing to hit the ground running and learn the job very, very quickly. I did this myself once when I was just barely 21. I had a full-time job that I could pretty much do in my sleep; I was single and had a lot of time on my hands. I went to a local restaurant to see if I could pick up a part-time waitress job. As it turned out, they didn't need any more waitresses at the time, but they were desperate for a bartender. They asked me if I had any experience. No. But could I learn to tend bar? Well, possibly. I started the next evening, a Thursday. The following night, a packed-wall-to-wall-and-drinking-like-fishes clientele were my initiation into the world of bartending. I ran that bar all by myself. It was a load of fun. Although I never learned to toss bottles the way bartenders are expected to do now to be trendy, nor did I ever actually dance on the bar, I did stay the better part of a year and was told that my drinks were excellent. I'm a little sad that our drinks had such tame names like martinis, margaritas, and daiquiris. Sex On The Beach just sounds so creatively challenging, but I digress.

Just making up your mind to change career directions isn't as easy as it sounds. You need to do your homework. You need to research employment fields that experts believe to be the growth industries. These are going to vary from state to state. Right now, in my state, these include IT technology, health care (CNA, LPN, RM, CMT, EMT), biosciences (EMT, phlebotomist), transportation (Class A CDL drivers), advanced manufacturing, HVAC (skilled technicians) and "Green" jobs (maintenance, solar energy and photovoltaics). You're going to have to go to a vocational/technical school, a college, or complete on-the-job training, but your challenge then is to find someone who will hire an educated-but-inexperienced newbie. It could happen. Is it likely? Hmm...like an asteroid hitting earth.

So, what should you do next in such an environment? Maybe do first things first by getting to better know yourself!

2

What Do You Want to Be When You Grow Up?

First Things First:
Choosing an Occupation

If you've been performing the same kind of work for a long time and the job market is stale (can you say "construction industry"?), you might want to change your career direction altogether. The biggest mistake that job seekers make in today's job market is to dash into their job searches without choosing an actual **goal**. The usual attitude is "I can do anything, I can learn anything, I'll *take anything!*" The really pertinent question, however, is "What do you want to be when you grow up?" Just as when you were young, you have to do your research to determine two major things: (1) What are your abilities and interests? and (2) Do these translate to a job that somebody will pay you to perform?

> ...
> **The really pertinent question is "What do you want to be when you grow up?"**
> ...

Not everyone starts out knowing just what they would be able to do well or what would really make them happy over time. As I said, desperation usually prevails at this point, and the "any-old-port-in-a-storm" mindset pushes people to grab the first available job opening they can lay hands on, without regard as to whether the job is one they actually desire or can perform with any degree of satisfaction over time. How many college students begin their academic career absolutely certain they want to be engineers, doctors, teachers, lawyers, only to discover that the road to that goal is far too long or much too expensive, the competition is too steep, or even that they really don't care for the field as much once they actually began studying it as when they first started those classes?

The same is true for seasoned job seekers. Many know they need a change in their occupations, but they really don't know how to get started or in what direction they should look for new purpose and possible guidance. Research is required, detailed research. It won't be easy, it's going to be predominantly self-directed, and therein lies the problem.

You're going to need at least a little bit of computer ability to do this, or access to a person who can assist you with this. My particular state has a website that lists economic data. I can't swear that all of the others do, but it's maintained by state government, so I can't imagine that it wouldn't be available in the other states. This website lists the top jobs that are considered in demand for particular regions of the state, not only today but projected into the future, maybe 10 years or so down the road. This should give you a sense of whether the field you've chosen to work in is going to provide the same rate of jobs as the present, or if the field will increase or diminish. Our website also shows the median rate of pay for those top jobs, to give you an idea of what the average person in one of those positions could expect to make per year. The site goes deeper into individual statistics and allows for searches for specific occupations.

The reason for all of this, of course, is to assist job seekers who want to train for a new career in making a sound decision based on good economic data. It's just not logical for someone to try to get into a career as, say, a blacksmith, since that's not going to be an in-demand career anywhere outside of Texas or Montana. Visit the economic website for your state and check out the data available to help you make an informed occupational decision.

> ...
> **Spend a little time performing an interest assessment that will help you determine what settings and functions you would really enjoy in your work environment.**
> ...

As part of that decision, spend a little time performing an **interest assessment** that will help you determine what settings and functions you would really enjoy in your work environment. One website that provides that interest assessment is www.onetonline.org. It's maintained by the federal government, and it offers a wealth of information, including job descriptions, to help job seekers research potential occupations. The interest assessment offered on that website is a slightly smaller version of some that are professionally available, but it's still an easy-to-use tool that individuals can take and interpret on their own with fairly accurate results.

Please, please do the necessary research before you abandon the occupational field you've been engaged in and strike off into the unknown. Make sure your decisions are based on sound data and good advice from workforce professionals. Go to your local Career Center (I'm positive your state will have them because my local workforce professionals organization is part of a national group) and talk to someone there to discuss training options. If you've been out of work for some time, you may be eligible for funding as a Dislocated Worker. Check on any and all student aid sources, and use them. Don't think that just because you're over 30, 40 or even 50 you can't learn a new trade.

> **...**
> **Make sure your decisions are based on sound data and good advice from professionals.**
> **...**

Old dogs **can** learn new tricks. They do it every day. Sit. Stay.

3
The New Realities

Like It or Not—This is How It Is

Those were good old days, weren't they? I mean the days when you could have a leisurely breakfast, open the newspaper to the want ads, scan all those juicy listings, close your eyes, jab your finger at a job, apply for it, and get it. Well, maybe it wasn't quite that easy, but it sure wasn't the pack-of-jackals-after-a-single-warthog-carcass that the job market is now.

Want Ads

Those want ads belong in the bottom of the birdcage. Want ad listings fall into two major categories: Bad Jobs and Scams.

Bad Jobs

The halfway legitimate jobs that are listed in want ads usually fall into the Bad Job genre. These are jobs that are either so incredibly specific that they can't be filled ("Wanted: Sales Representative specializing in surgical equipment, payroll administration, and structural analysis of multi-level commercial buildings; belly dancer preferred") or they're actual jobs that nobody wants (replenishing paper supplies in port-a-potties).

Scam Jobs

Then there are the Scam Jobs. You probably know what I'm talking about here. I've had clients sit at my desk and sob about losing money in one job scam or another. They all have the same components: You provide Company X with your credit card number, which they will charge for X dollars, and Company X will then provide you a computer and a database, and you will contact the individuals in their database and read whatever the provided script says you should read to them. You will then make X dollars per month by working at home in your jammies and your bunny slippers, and you will eventually become independently wealthy without ever leaving the comfort of your own home. You never get the computer or the database, but you do get charged for the X dollars on your credit card, and you thank your lucky stars that it was only X dollars instead of XXX dollars. There must be a special place in hell (perhaps the X level) for scam artists who take advantage of single-parent moms or retirees who get sucked into these schemes. If there isn't, there ought to be.

> ...
> **The #1 way to land a job these days is through networking.**
> ...

Networking

The #1 way to land a job these days is through networking. This includes three distinct venues: job clubs, job fairs, and personal contacts.

1. Job Clubs

Job clubs are groups of people who meet in community facilities—usually church basements—to discuss their job search efforts and to exchange information about what companies they've applied to, received feedback from, or just heard rumors about regarding impending hiring or layoff events. You don't have to belong to the specific churches to attend these events. The denominations usually make their facilities available as a service to their communities.

If you want to get together with a nice group of people who want to share the misery of today's job market and maybe a few lemon bars, by all means, go to a job club. Take with you the patience of Job (the biblical one) because the stories you're going to hear are going to bum you out even more than you were when you walked into the building. These are mostly support groups. Who's getting "supported"—at least emotionally—isn't clear. I have yet to hear of anyone who has actually landed a job from a tip they received at a job club. As I understand it, the only group to really benefit from these get-togethers is the local Weight Watchers organizations. Permanence is also a problem. These job clubs pop up and close down on an unpredictable basis, so as soon as a list of locations rolls off the printer, it's usually obsolete.

> ...
> **Job clubs pop up and close down on an unpredictable basis.**
> ...

2. Job Fairs

Job fairs! Oh, yes, job fairs! Don't you love those things? What is a job fair? Technically, it's a meeting in a big room, like a convention room, filled with long tables covered with pretty tablecloths with company names and lots of brochures and paperwork about individual corporations on them. Behind the tables are disinterested but tastefully attired business representatives who would much rather be at their desks in their offices, reading the *Wall Street Journal* or checking their email, possibly even their business email. Instead, they drew the short straws that made it mandatory for them to represent their companies to a bunch of people they probably either don't need to hire or don't want to hire in the first place. They are putting their corporate faces out there because they need to keep good public relations going in the remote event that the economy will turn around to the degree that they have to hire more employees instead of "downsizing" employees coming perilously close to retirement with full benefits. Pick up their brochures and their free ink pens, hand the surly professionals your resume, answer the few questions they may deign to ask you, and chalk it up to getting a little interview experience. Don't go out and buy your new business wardrobe just yet.

> ...
> **Some specialized job fairs include enthusiastic representatives who really work for scarce talent.**
> ...

On the other hand, some specialized job fairs (focus on a particular skill sought or occupational group, such as information technology, nursing, transitioning military, and security-clearance only intelligence) include enthusiastic representatives who really work the job fair for scarce talent. Such operations often witness job interviews and offers, even at the job fair! So standing in line with a great resume and looking and behaving like a professional at one of these events could have unexpected results, such as a job interview that quickly leads to a job offer!

3. Personal Contacts

Personal contacts are by far the **best** way to get your foot in the door somewhere. Everybody has four different personal networks: family and friends, professional contacts, community contacts, and what I will refer to as fortuitous accidents, although they're technically called opportunistic relationships by people who teach this stuff.

Family and Friends

The first group is obvious. Your brother has an auto body shop and you like to work with your hands and maybe you know how to, or can learn to, fix dents. Joe Bob can put you to work in his business, or maybe he knows of somebody he deals with that might need some help. You've remained friends with some of the people you went to school with, and now they have businesses in the community. You play poker on Friday nights with a guy whose brother needs some help doing this job or the other in his business, hopefully, legally.

Professional Contacts

Professional contacts are the professionals you deal with, such as doctors, dentists, lawyers, probation officers, and pastors. In the course of an office call from you, they might tell you about a job opening they heard about from another of their patients/clients/whatevers. If it's not a violation of their professional-client relationship, they might be able to give you a useful tip.

Community Contacts

Community contacts are just what they sound like: groups or individuals in your community. We're talking Boy Scouts, Girl Scouts, Little League, PTA, Chamber of

Commerce, homeowners' associations, that kind of organization. If your child goes to Scouts, you might get to know the parents of some of his or her friends through going to those group meetings. Through this kind of fraternization, you might be able to make job contacts that will help get you interviews or at least be alerted when potential hirings might occur.

Fortuitous Accidents

Accidents. Some people don't believe in accidents. They believe that everything is already written in stone and nothing happens without a reason. Without standing on my personal soapbox about this, I'll just call these events "fortuitous accidents" and say, yes, they happen every day. They've happened to me and changed my life. A fortuitous accident is sort of a moment in time when you just happen to be in the right place at the right time, and you meet the exact right person who can make a decision or put you in touch with the person who can. I'm convinced that we all end up in exactly the place we're supposed to be, performing exactly the work we're intended to do (at least at that moment), and sometimes a fortuitous accident brings that about. It's not scientific, and, no, I don't have statistics to back it up. It's like Santa Claus. You either believe in its possibility and are open to it when it happens, or you're not.

And then there is the biggest monster of them all in the job searching universe: The Internet.

The Internet

Drum roll, please. The Internet! Experts state that, of all jobs listed anywhere—in print media, electronic media, job clubs, job placement agencies, fliers nailed on the sides of telephone poles, etc.—80 percent are actually listed in an Internet web-site, either a job search engine like Monster or CareerBuilder or a company website. "Okay," you say, "I knew that." But did you know that, of those Internet-listed jobs, those same experts say that less than 12 percent of those jobs are actually filled by applications placed through those sites?

Why do you suppose that is? It's easily answered. Most of the jobs placed on those websites are already earmarked for current employees or hand-picked candidates, and the listings are just placed on the website to meet EEOC require-ments. Companies go through the motions of posting these fabulous opportunities to prevent lawsuits. Get excited about an Internet listing if you want to, and by all means apply for it, but realize that your chances resemble that proverbial ice cube in the nether regions and it's still about networking. Networking. Say it after me: Networking. Good. Now say it like you mean it.

So, in the world of work, what does this mean for you? It means that jobs clubs and jobs fairs are often Loser Ac-tivities and the Internet is a great place to do occupation-al research, play video games, and chat with people you haven't seen in many years, but reaching out to influential people is still the real way to find an actual job. I'm not talk-ing about going door to door, from company to company. They're not going to talk to you anyway. If you show up un-announced at the HR department, you will pretty much kill any chances you might have had of finding employment there. No, what I'm talking about is finding out the names of movers and shakers from people who might be able to introduce you properly, people who can send you to that company with a legitimate referral so you will be received. That's done through networks. Use them.

4

Love Them or Hate Them, Computers Rule

You Can't Avoid Them Anymore

How can you even doubt it? Look around you. They're everywhere, and every single day we live, there's another use for a technology advancement to run some facet of our world that we never dreamed—or feared—possible.

I remember my father being petrified when grocery stores first introduced scanners to ring item prices into the registers. It was clearly the "Mark of the Beast" come into our reality to enslave us. I must admit to thinking there might be some truth to that because my father was the smartest man I had ever known (he had a seventh grade education and went on to teach himself Greek so he could read the Septuagint Bible!) and if he said this was the Beginning of the End, it certainly must be. Life went on and no one came and took us away, so we came to accept the grocery scanners into our lives with little fanfare.

Scanners led to our being issued bank cards, and didn't those just scare the living daylights out of you? They sure did my family! Once again, it was the coming of the Anti-Christ and the beginning of the One-World Government. As long as no one showed up with a branding iron to stamp the number of the Beast on our hands or foreheads, we let it pass and learned to live with bank cards.

Our video games evolved from little plastic console boxes that played limited games to complex plastic console boxes that could also play movies, run your exercise program, tell you how to prepare dinner, and probably put the laundry in the washer if you would just ask it nicely. The point is, our entertainment systems became more and more sophisticated, paving the way for our cell phones to become all-powerful and to take control of every facet of our day-to-day lives, as they now do. Just 10 years ago, my husband could not have conceived of the possibility that he would spend more time chatting with his friends on his cell phone than I do.

I'll never forget the battle royal that ensued when I came home one wintry day and told him that my boss had slid off of a snow-packed road into a ditch, and she was unable to get any of her car doors open to get out of the vehicle. She was trapped inside, in a rural area, where, without traffic going by and without any way for family or friends to know where she was, she would probably have been forced to eat the stuffing out of the seat cushions for sustenance. She had, however, thought to bring along a little device that she had that I had never seen before: a portable telephone! Using that incredible life-saver, she was able to summon help to get her out of the ditch. I was in complete awe. Not of her, just the telephone. After she showed me that tiny little six-inch-long and three-inch-thick piece of portable security blanket, I swore I would have one, too, and I did, the very same day.

When I got home, my husband and I rationally discussed my need for a portable telephone. He couldn't fathom why anyone would need to carry a telephone around with them, notwithstanding the story of the car and the ditch and eating the seat cushions. It was just stupid. It was unnecessary. It was expensive. Why did I...? Why did I...? What was I thinking?

Flash forward to today. My husband uses his cell phone(s) daily, for work and for social chit chat with his buddies. I, on the other hand, have to talk on the phone at work all day. I avoid telephones of any variety, be they landlines, cellular, satellite, or intracranial (which, I'm sure, will be the next tele-communications breakthrough). The majority of us text, IM, podcast, blog, and tweet our brains out on a daily basis. Our addiction with all things Internet isn't even news anymore. If you walk through a mall, I guarantee you that every teenager, female and male alike, will be texting as they move, with little regard for any activity going on around them – that is, if they don't just have a cell phone growing out of their ear in the first place or if they're not glued to their iPad or iPod. And it's not just teenagers! It's all of us! It's middle-aged people, seniors on walkers, below-the-knees rugrats racing through the crowds, eyes on their electronic babysitter.

> ...
> **The majority of us text, IM, podcast, blog, and tweet our brains out on a daily basis.**
> ...

The point I'm trying to make is, one day we've never heard of a piece of technology and the next day we can't live without it. That's what happened with computers. Those of you who thought they were only a fad need to realize there is no turning back. Computers rule! Try booking a plane ticket, paying a bill, watching your television, buying a car, driving a car....Computers rule the world.

They're probably not evil, at least not yet. Whether they are or not, we need to make friends with them in order to live our lives. To do that, we have to learn to operate them. Most community colleges offer basic computer classes at reasonable prices. Basic classes usually introduce you to the Mouse, the Keyboard, the CPU (central processing unit), the Monitor (the TV-screen-type thing), and Windows (the operating environment). (Don't even ask me about the Mac system; it may actually BE evil!) The point is, one of these basic classes can teach you everything you need to know to become computer if-not-savvy-at-least-partially-acquainted. You'll be able to understand enough to do basic job research and probably communicate with the world through email, two activities that are essential in the modern job search world. Unless you want to hold a job that requires specific computer skills, that's enough to maneuver through the modern job-seeking landscape.

> ...
> **Most community colleges offer basic computer classes at reasonable prices. One of these basic classes can teach you everything you need to know to become computer if-not-savvy-at-least-partially-acquainted.**
> ...

These same community colleges also offer more advanced classes in specific applications, like Word, Excel, PowerPoint, Access, Quicken, and whatever programs are in vogue by the time this book goes to press. There are also tutorials that can be found (free, usually) online that can help you learn the basics of these programs, once you get comfortable with the basics of computer usage. To use what you learn from these tutorials, though, you're going to need access to a computer that has these software packages loaded. Career centers have some of them; libraries do, also. Practice, practice, practice, before you list these skills on your resume. If you list them, you **must** be able to demonstrate them!

I must make one other point about computers. I'm not going to mention the actual name I have in mind, but be very, very wary of what websites you utilize in your job search. Stick with sites that are time-tested and proven to be legitimate and secure. You probably know the ones I'm talking about here: Monster and CareerBuilder are the giants among websites and the pillars of the Internet community. Others aren't as big and may be a little more specific as to what clientele they are geared for (ani malsciencejobs.com, for instance, designed for people wanting to work with animals), but they are still tried-and-true and have loyal followings. Most of these are considered user-friendly and contain good quality job listings.

> ...
> **Be very, very wary of what websites you utilize in your job search. Stick with sites that are time-tested and proven to be legitimate and secure.**
> ...

And then there are some others, like, shall we say, "Geek's List" (name changed to protect the author.) I have friends who have sold cars and bought horses (honestly!) on this particular website, and they swear by their good experiences. I have also had numerous clients who have come to my desk to ask me how to go about getting back the money they spent on scam job offers or the steps they need to take to sanitize their stolen identity. The problem is a simple one. You would think that common sense would prevail, but it apparently doesn't when people are computer neophytes. They find an attractive job listing on this website. The job reads like something they could do. They're asked to email their resume to an email address. The email address is something like joebobdannyboy@ somewebsite.com. There is no company name mentioned. They are expected to submit their resumes, containing their personal information, to an email address they don't even recognize. For all they know, their resumes could be put into use by Renaldo SomethingSpanish, sitting at a cyber-café somewhere in Argentina, where he is generating fake IDs. Identity theft is the newest industry for criminals seeking to upgrade their own job skills. Don't go there. Don't contribute to their new vocational success.

> ...
> **It's actually much harder for you to hurt a computer than for a computer to hurt you.**
> ...

Stick with safe, secure sites or stay offline. It's actually much harder for you to hurt a computer than for a computer to hurt you. If you get into a site you don't understand or aren't comfortable with, the ESCAPE key will always be your best friend.

5
Send My Computer Your Resume

All That Resume Stuff—Styles, Objectives, References, Keywords, and, Oh, Yeah, Honesty

Now let's get into the really essential tool for job searching: resumes. You probably already have one. The problem is, you need a different one. I can say that without even seeing the one you've already carefully crafted. Why is that? You're unemployed, aren't you? Unless you have really extenuating circumstances—like not actually looking for a job or blowing the interview if and when you get one—the reason you're not working is probably because your resume looks just like everybody else's in the continental United States and some parts of Asia. I'll bet I can describe it for you. (This is technical, long and tedious. Go get yourself a Coke right now, make a trip to the bathroom, turn the ringer down on the phone, and get comfortable. Ready? Okay, here we go!)

> ...
> **You probably already have one. The problem is, you need a different one.**
> ...

Resume Structure and Tips

It has your contact information at the top, usually in the center, followed by a really, really vague Objective. This objective is supposed to state, in a brief sentence, what you can bring to the table if a company hires you. I'll bet it doesn't, though.

I'll bet it reads more like what you want the company to do for you. "Experienced administrative clerical office specialist, seeking an opportunity to utilize my skills and education in a progressive company that offers benefits and the opportunity for advancement." And let's don't forget a great cafeteria!

Then you've got the section called "Work Experience" where you list every single job you've held since you mowed lawns back in middle school, starting, of course, with your most recent job first, then the one before that, then the one before that, then the one before…This is called the reverse-chronological resume.

You list the city and state where the company was located, your job title there, and the dates you started and left the company. Then you probably go one of two ways: Either you have a hundred-word paragraph that describes exactly what you did on each job, right down to the times you took your lunch breaks, or you don't describe anything about the job at all. You let it stand all by itself, as if the reader would intuitively know what you did at that company by the company name itself.

The next section is most likely a tabulated list of skills that you want the reader to know that you possess. You may have looked at a directory or database of skills that workers might potentially have, and you just listed as many of them as you recognized. Of course, if you get an interview, you're going to have to be able to discuss these skills and where you gained them, but don't they look good, all lined up like that?

Your education is way down there at the bottom of the page. It might be a high school diploma, a GED, or maybe vocational training. It's really close to the bottom of the page because it's been so long ago that you really don't want to talk about it. You've probably even listed the year you graduated. Wow, that has been a minute ago, hasn't it?

The last entry I see on your resume is a line that says "References available upon request," or you may have even listed your three best friends, your three closest relatives, or former supervisors that you know don't even work for those companies anymore and are therefore unreachable.

I'm going to file your resume with all the others I've looked at today. Bzzzzzzz….Uh-oh, excuse me for a minute, I've got to go empty the shredder.

Let's look at how people used to get jobs BC, before computers. You filled out an application, left it with the receptionist, and somebody called you, right? This meant that somebody had looked your application over and decided that you had a stable work history, that you said that you had the skills the company needed, and that your penmanship was good enough to let them read your home phone number and call you in for an interview. You went in to the interview and said the right things and they hired you. Easy as that, 1-2-3.

When companies began to have so many applications to scrutinize that they couldn't handle them anymore, resumes became mandatory. Now you had to write a formally structured list of where you've worked, what you knew how to do, and where you went to school. You used to have to list references on the resume until it became apparent that all of your references had your same last name.

This reverse-chronological resume was uniform. You might type it on pastel paper or go wild and use Helvetica instead of Times New Roman font, but, damn it, the structure had to be the same as everyone else's! No originality allowed. So all resumes looked pretty much the same for, oh, I don't know, 20 years?

The relatives of the hiring manager, Sammy Jo Johnson, had to type resumes, too, but those resumes still found themselves on top of the interview stack and those relatives still got hired while apparently qualified candidates were turned away. Hmm, how to fix this? Why not make it so that neither Sammy Jo nor any other person could decide who got called in for interviews? Neither applications nor paper resumes would be the determining factors anymore. We could take the human factor completely out of the equation. Enter computer filtering programs and the importance of keywords.

> ...
> **Keywords are words that are associated with the performance of a specific job.**
> ...

For those who don't know, **keywords** are words that are associated with the performance of a specific job. In other words, if I'm a welder and I'm writing a resume for a welder, I want to reference words that indicate my skills as a welder. I'm going to need to be able to list that I can do *MIG* welding, *TIG* welding, *structural* welding, *aluminum* welding, and *pipe* welding.

Computers know this. For the job description "welder," the database may list these five words. That means, when the computer looks at a resume, it's going to expect to see these five words mentioned in the applicant's job experience. For each mention of one of those words, the computer is going to issue a point (score!). If the computer expects to find an acceptable score of five for the ideal welder, and I only use four of those words, my score will be four and I may or may not get the "thanks-but-no-thanks" letter. If I have all five, I may get the letter asking me to contact HR to set up my interview.

Computers became all-powerful, as we now know them to be. Software packages would open online employment applications and look at the uploaded resumes, issuing scores for how many job-specific keywords were referenced in the documents. Most people didn't know about the omnipotent Keyword Police, and so, for many years, they didn't know why they weren't getting jobs, even though their resumes were appropriately reverse-chronological and replete with impressive employment references.

Guess what? The Keyword Police are still in action. If your resume isn't getting the responses you hoped for, look at the keywords that should be present in your resume. If they're not there, put them there. Use as many keywords as you can legitimately claim. Realize, however, that in addition to listing them on your resume, you're going to have to be able to discuss them. But a caveat: if you list 30 keywords, the computer looking at your resume is going to assume you're just copying words out of a book and eliminate you from the list of candidates. See what I mean? They really are the Keyword Police and they're determined to keep you honest!

> ...
> **If your resume isn't getting the responses you hoped for, look at the keywords that should be present in your resume. If they're not there, put them there.**
> ...

So, this is the way people get jobs today. They write a really kick-butt resume, using the appropriate style and structure, applying legitimate and meaningful keywords, in order to get the attention of the computer that will determine their worthiness of an interview. Then they go to the interview, and, hopefully, don't blow it.

We're not ready yet to discuss the interview. We are not done talking about resumes. What should a good resume look like today? I've already told you that the reverse-chronological style is somewhat dated, boring, unimaginative, and unimpressive. The style of resume that is the most effective is the **functional resume**. This style of resume flip-flops the two sections where the employment history and the skills list or summary usually occurs.

> ...
> **The reverse-chronological style is somewhat dated, boring, unimaginative, and unimpressive.**
> ...

The order of the functional resume would be something like this:

Contact Information

Name, Address, Home Phone Number, Cell Phone Number, Email Address. This goes at the top as usual. I prefer centered. Use whatever looks esthetically pleasing to you. All of our resumes don't actually have to look alike, after all. They just need to make an awesome impression in 10 seconds or less. And, speaking of an awesome impression, how much more awesome an impression could you make than if you list an email address like BgDong@Webserver.com or HapyHo4U@Webserver.net? Think, people! The email address you list on your resume is going to say something about you, and what you don't want it to say is your hourly rate or your personal fetish. Change your email ID to something dull, boring, appropriate. Maybe use your name.

Objective

Use an Objective only if the job you are looking for is so specific that you wouldn't consider anything else ("Biochemical Engineer," for example). Most people's Objectives are meaningless.

Professional Summary, or Abilities Summary, or Skills Summary

The Professional Summary lists who you are (professional roles) and the Abilities Summary or Skills Summary lists what you know how to do. As an example, in a Professional Summary, I might list this:

- Manager of staff of 12 accounting professionals

- Writer of regular community newsletter, pamphlets, and brochures

- Sales representative for national pharmacy chain

If I want to use the Abilities Summary or Skills Summary, I would list something like this:

- Produced annual report for submission to Corporate Office

- Ran variety of office machines, including copiers, scanner, fax machine, multi-line telephone, and computer

- Loaded and unloaded incoming produce on loading dock

I might bullet each line with a cute little bit of art to set it off, or I might not. It's a matter of choice. The point is, use one style or the other. If you use the Professional Summary, you're using nouns; if you use the Skills Summary, you're using verbs. Be consistent.

List all of the information you think an employer might want to know about your **abilities**. This is a laundry list. You're not going to indicate on what job you gained each experience. You'll list employers further down the page, and you can discuss in person where you performed certain tasks. For the moment, you want the interviewer to see in one place a list of the reasons why they need you. You want them to see the diversity of your experience and the good stuff you can contribute to their company. Brainstorm and make a list of everything you know how to do in an employment setting, whether you got paid for it or not. If you did volunteer work, that work experience still counts. Make your list. Go over it again and again, consolidating lines that can be combined. Make this list read like credits you would want on your tombstone. Use only your best stuff.

Work Experience

Those "experts" I mentioned earlier will tell you not to list employment that goes back further than 10 years. Don't listen to them. If you held a job in the past that is relevant to the job you're seeking now, list it anyway, because I'm going to go out on a limb here and recommend that you **don't use dates on your resume**. When you fill out actual job applications, you'll have to list dates, and then an interviewer can nail you on how long ago that job has been, in which case you'll explain how that job was important in preparing you for the job you are seeking. But right now, we're writing a resume to get you the interview in the first place.

Under the Work History section, you're going to list the names of the companies, the cities and states where they were located, and your actual job titles for those companies. That's all. You're not going to list a synopsis of what you did at those companies (all of those things should be up above in the Professional Summary or Skills Summary). This is just a list. That's all. You'll discuss what you did at these companies in your interview. No dates! Pop quiz: Are we using dates? No!

Education/Certification

You'll list your high school diploma, the name of the high school you graduated from, the city and state. You will not list the year. Let's don't give anybody a reason to not interview you because you're...well, you know, older.

If you have a GED (General Equivalency Diploma), you list GED and the state in which it was issued. Again, are we listing the year...?

If you have college degrees, you'll want to lead off the Education section with those because, after all, you want to hit them with your most impressive credentials. What did I say about GPA? Don't bother to list it, please. Nobody cares. List the name of the institution, city, state, degree, discipline. No year.

References

A word about References: Nu-uh! In the old days, the line "References available upon request" was always listed at the bottom of the resume. It was the resume version of "Amen." A resume wasn't complete without it. Don't do it. As I've said earlier, it is a foregone conclusion by employers that if you are asked to provide references, you can and will. These references are not going to be your family, your friends, or names chosen out of a telephone book. Human Resources people will probably ask you to provide the names, addresses, and telephone numbers of recent supervisors you've worked under, or of individuals you know in a professional capacity, which could include co-workers as long as they can be shown to be peers, not just drinking buddies.

> ...
> **The functional resume is an easier resume for an interviewer to read and evaluate.**
> ...

Easy on the Eyes

The functional resume is an easier resume for an interviewer to read and evaluate. In the world of art, there is a concept referred to as "the rule of thirds." What it says is that our eye naturally is drawn to the center of a picture or painting. The same is true for a document. If you're used to looking at papers all day long, you tend to skip over contact information and objectives and you go straight for the goodies in the middle of the page. This is the center third our eyes are geared to focus on. This is also where you want to put the information that you most want a screener to see. You only have 10 seconds or so for your document to make an impression. If you list company/function, then another company/function, then another...and so on, the reader may see what you did for one single employer. They will not see the sum total of what you have to offer. This is why the Professional Summary or Skills Summary is so important. This is in that sacred center third where the eye will focus for those critical 10 seconds. Make the most of it.

Honesty

Last, but not least, let's talk about honesty. Highly acclaimed writer, brilliant humor columnist, and author of the book *Claw Your Way To The Top*, Dave Barry may have said it best when he noted, "A resume is a piece of paper covered with lies...." Unfortunately, a vast number of resumes making their way onto HR desks these days are just that. The competition is so keen for any and all jobs, and some people believe that with thousands of job applicants competing for the same jobs, that companies won't take the time to completely check out all the details listed on applications and on resumes. Guess again! They will. It will just take some time.

We live in an age now where checks of all kinds are a standard part of virtually all aspects of our lives. We have credit checks, driving record checks, background checks, security screening checks, blood pressure checks, cholesterol and colon screening checks…you name it and they've got it. We have been scanned so far up the wazzoo that we tend to take such screenings for granted.

As far as employment is concerned, when you are hired by a company, you will almost always have to sign a document giving them authorization to conduct a background check. If you opt out of it, of course, you also opt out of your chance at employment with that company, so you sign the form and forget about it.

The next thing that happens is the investigator contracted by the company will start making inquiries with the employers you said you worked for in the past. Legally, there are certain things they can ask, but we all know that sometimes information filters out from personnel records that we might not be comfortable with. The investigator will gather as much employment history as possible, usually conduct a credit check, and, depending on the kind of work you're going to be doing, also do a criminal background check.

I worked as a Security Screener at an airport where, six months after completing the training, a co-worker of mine was called into the office and fired because her credit check came back bad. The rationale was that she was in a position to check personal baggage of airline travelers, off-camera, and that, if her credit was bad and she needed money to pay debts, she might be inclined to steal money, jewelry, or other valuables from checked baggage. We, her co-workers, were appalled, not that she would be fired for that reason (although we were sure she would never commit such an act), but that they had taken so long to act on the credit check. Such is the way these things move today. Just when you get comfy, feeling secure, BAM!!!

If you have lied about anything on your application or on your resume, rest assured, you will be found out. Don't lie, don't exaggerate, don't embellish. Tell the truth, nothing but the truth. It's just not worth the aggravation to try to get by with background you haven't earned.

> ...
> **Don't lie, don't exaggerate, don't embellish. Tell the truth, nothing but the truth.**
> ...

Error Free and Saved

Your resume should be the best picture of you that it can be. It should be spelled **correctly.** Use "spellcheck"! Nothing could be more embarrassing than to list your position as Shift Manager and you leave the "f" out! Your grammar should be good. Have a friend, or friends, read what you've written to make sure it sounds good and is easy to understand. Make it visually pleasing, centered on the page. DON'T PUT EVERYTHING IN CAPS! Caps is the type-written version of yelling. Don't **bold** everything. **If you bold everything, then nothing stands out.** Bold only your name and section headers.

Save your resume on a flash drive and on a hard drive. It's never safe to save your document in only one place. You can craft a different resume for each of several different kinds of jobs if you really want to, but if you make a functional resume, you probably won't need to.

Your resume is you. Make it something you can be proud of.

6

Cover Letters?

Yes, You Need Them, Even With an Online Application—Just How Gushy Should They Be?

I'm sending my resume to your company to show you that I can work really good and I'll do any kind of work you got. It don't really matter cause I just need a job to pay my bills and I ain't worked since my sister Ruth Ann moved in with all her kids last year and I sure couldn't leave the house to get no job cause otherwise they'd steal me blind. But she got picked up for shoplifting and those Family Services people got the kids, so I can leave the house now. I really want to work for your company and I won't leave and go to work for nobody else not even if they ask me to cause I'd much rather pack doorknobs on your assembly line than flip them burgers over at Pokey's Diner. Call me. Thanks."

Since text-messaging became a way of life, I've gotten out of the habit of writing letters. Well, to be perfectly honest, I've never been much on writing letters in the first place because I come from a background and profession where anything you put on paper can be held against you in a court of law. So, writing is a thing done of necessity, not for pleasure.

Still, the reality is, people in a corporate setting have certain expectations. They have a certain protocol that they expect job candidates to exercise. Letter-writing is one of them: cover letters, thank you letters after interviews, and, God willing, acceptance letters.

There is a virtual plethora of letters that are considered standard-issue in the corporate world. We're not going to talk about all of them here because, unless you become some kind of Administrative Something, you're not going to need them. You are going to need to master the intricacies of the **cover letter**.

> ...
> **People in a corporate setting have certain expectations. Letter-writing is one of them.**
> ...

It isn't brain surgery. Nobody expects you to have any kind of fancy, personalized letterhead paper. An online cover letter is even easier to write because you don't even have to worry about paper. The structure of the regular cover letter is the same as any other letter.

Cover Letter Structure

(First line) your name; (next line) your street address; (next line) your city, state and zip code; (next line) telephone number; and (next line) email address (keep it professional, please).

Skip about four lines. On the next line, you list the date you're writing the letter.

Skip a line. On the next line, type the name of the business you're applying to; (next line) the street address; (next line) the city, state and zip code.

Skip a line. Type "Sirs:" (without the quotation marks).

Skip a line. You have now reached the body of the letter. Don't tell them your life story. Tell them why you're sending your resume. My preferred cover letter would go something like this:

"As a (Job Title), I am very interested in the job opening you listed on (Website). With __ years' experience in the field, I've gained the skills necessary to contribute significantly in that capacity.

I believe you'll find from my attached resume that I would be a real asset to your company. Thank you for your consideration."

Skip a line. Type "Respectfully," (again, without the quotation marks).

Skip about four more lines. Type your name.

Print it out as well as your resume. Type out an envelope. Put both pieces of paper in the envelope. Place a postage stamp in the upper righthand corner. Mail the envelope. Go have a Coke. You're done.

That's a **Paper Cover Letter**. But, wait, there's more! Bonus! It's also an **Online Cover Letter**!

You can use the very same cover letter template in the cover letter box you'll usually find in online applications. You know what I'm talking about: There's a box where the application will ask for you to upload your resume. You'll usually upload that from your little flash drive or your hard drive. Then just a little bit further down on the application, there might be a box that asks you to upload or type your cover letter. This is a hard-and-fast rule: If there is a box for a cover letter, that means the company expects to find one! Do not leave that box blank! This is a test. If you leave the

> ...
> **If there is a box for a cover letter, that means the company expects to find one!**
> ...

box blank, the company will assume (1) you have absolutely no attention to detail whatsoever and you just missed seeing the box in the first place, or (2) you're hoping to skate on the merits of your application and resume alone, and you don't think you can (or don't want to) communicate with them in letter form. Use this same form letter in the little box. Just be sure to personalize it for the appropriate company.

Candy, Flowers, Bribes?

I once actually worked for a company that valued extreme creativity. I won't mention it by name, but we'll just say it was a major mid-western greeting card company and let it go at that. They expected outrageous bursts of inventiveness from their job candidates. For instance, a writer who was hoping to work for this company used a huge heart-shaped box of Valentine candy and, instead of the usual ingredients listing on the bottom of the box, the writer plastered it with samples of his original work. A product designer used a tin soup can, and created his own product label, then filled the can with little trinkets representing his product ideas, sealed it back up, and sent it to the Creative Recruiter.

I've heard of other instances where candidates have sent those huge, personalized cookies to Human Resources representatives in an effort to seal the deal, and yet other cases where out-and-out bribes were on the table. Let's be realistic here. They're working. You're not. Do you really have so much money that the folding currency you could slide across that desk would impress them? I doubt it. Keep it for the cable bill.

7

Social Networking

So That's What You Do With
Your Saturday Nights!

I f you get a chance this weekend, IM (Instant Message) me on Facebook. Yeah, I hang out online a lot, especially on the weekends. Oh, you know, it's a good way to keep up with what all my old friends from home are doing now, and, besides, I've met a couple of really nice guys on this one adult networking site and we're having text-sex. Yeah, all of us....Well, not at the same time. You know, me and Dave one time, then me and Todd another time. No, they don't know about each other, why would they? They're in separate states. It's just on the Net, you know. It's not for real. Does my husband know? Well, no, but why would he care? Like I said, it's not real, and besides, it doesn't matter what I do as long as he gets dinner and beer and the TV is on. Oh, yeah, did you see the pictures I posted of Kathy's party? There's a really good one of all of us together, toasting. Toasting, you know, raising our drink glasses...."

...
Companies stalk potential job candidates on the Internet to see how they behave in their "real" lives.
...

The above monologue isn't illegal; it may be slightly immoral, but it most definitely could be extremely damaging to your career hopes and aspirations. How? Get ready, this may be a surprise.

Companies are now employing Human Resources people to perform one major function: To stalk potential job candidates on the Internet to see how they behave in their "real" lives.

It isn't enough to have a fabulous resume with an impeccable job history. It isn't enough to have the perfect education and unimpeachable references. In addition to background checks that must come back spotless, your private life must be squeaky clean online as well. The corporate web-stalker—let's call him your Internet Ghost—is empowered to Google your name to find out which social networking sites you frequent, and then to track you there. The Ghost will read your profile, scrutinize your photos (don't raise those drink glasses too high or look like you're enjoying it too much!), and even, possibly, Google and check out some of your listed Friends. The object is, of course, to find out if the real you has any correlation to the paper you.

> ...
> **Your private life must be squeaky clean online as well.**
> ...

Who have you "friended" (invited to join your network) recently? Do you even know what I'm talking about? Okay, let me give you a quick overview of social sites like Facebook and MySpace (although all of my actual, personal experience is from Facebook; I *farm*).

A social network on the Internet is a website dedicated to the coming together online of people and their friends, acquaintances, and complete strangers who share a common interest in specific topics, media, games, activities, or people. Whole websites are created, dedicated to these activities. Some allow people to compete with other gamers in an online venue; some are designed to raise the praises of activities or causes; and some are just there to showcase naked bodies. (We call these last ones "porn," in case you don't know.)

Example: I said I *farm*. I don't actually farm in dirt. I play an online game called "Farmville." It's a game that can only be played on Facebook because Facebook created and hosts it. In this game, I build and develop a little graphically depicted farm, where I plant little graphic crops and raise little graphic animals. The game requires the cooperation of friends, which means I must solicit the help of my online friends to fertilize my fields, feed my chickens and perform other digitally based farm chores, and in order to progress in the game, I must perform the same tasks for them. Hence, the social aspect. You must interact by sending each other messages, checking each other's "walls," and in the process, you come to know a great deal about other people and their lives. It's a highly addictive game. I warn you: This is Computer Crack! If you don't have lots and lots of time to devote to it, don't even start it. I've tried playing "Mafia Wars" and "Frontierville," but they just didn't give me the sense of achievement that I reached when I hit Level 89 and could then send friends gifts of more than just digital cows and sheep. Mangrove trees are always popular. What a rush!

> ...
> **A social network on the Internet is a website dedicated to the coming together online of people who share a common interest.**
> ...

I have known of some of my "friends" who have actually met online, come to know each other online, then arranged to meet in the real world and went on to get married. Such are the stories of true love in the new century: People getting to know people based on the lies they tell on their home pages. Marriages are made of some of these and some marriages are known to end based on the same media. A friend of mine pursued an online relationship with someone she met on an "adult" social website where they hooked up and just talked dirty with each other, but her husband found out and frowned on the activity. This led on to other yet more sordid revelations, and eventually the marriage failed. Who can say whether the social network was to blame, but it sure didn't help.

My point is this: If I were applying to a company for a job and the Internet Ghost tracked me back to my Facebook farm and saw the excessive number of hours I spend in my digital dirt, they might get the idea that I am shallow or immature, not worthy of a position in their sophisticated midst. The same assumption might be true if they saw entries I might write for my friends to see on MySpace. If they saw that I was "following"[1] Jimmy Buffet and the Coral Reefers on Twitter, they would rightly assume that I was a Parrot-head and decide they wouldn't hire me simply because they don't approve of my choice of music and they might infer certain things from the lifestyle they might believe goes along with being a Parrot-head. (Parrot-heads have been known to hoist a few margaritas from time to time!) They might notice that one of my passions is the preservation of Second Amendment

---

[1] Another form of "friending" but usually with people you don't stand a chance in hell of even meeting in real life, such as celebrities. You can "follow" them and they share their thoughts on anything and everything, as well as comments they may make about how tough it is to be a celebrity, with all of these people wanting to know about every detail of their lives, and, of course, a blow-by-blow description of the events of their day. You can also "follow" regular people, so you can find out what room of the house they're in at this very moment, whether they've had dinner yet, and if they are even wearing clothing. But why would you want to know?

rights and thus wrongfully believe that I must be some kind of anarchist or terrorist because of my interest in guns. I really just love target-shooting, but they won't know that.

Clean up your Internet profiles on those social networks. Keep your messages clean and grammatically correct. Only post pictures of you and yours fully clothed, preferably taken by a professional studio. Watch what information you disclose—likes and dislikes, the history of other websites you've visited—and make sure you always, always look corporate online. Please keep this in mind for the time **after** you get the job, if you get it: don't ever, ever, ever criticize an employer— former, potential, current or otherwise—on the Internet. The Internet Ghost will find out and your career will be over.

Dominus no-biscuits. Welcome to your new saintly life.

8

Call Me, Okay?

How Your Telephone Can be the Death of Your Career

Communication in this new century has just gotten completely out of control. I can't believe we were meant to go around with our heads constantly attached to a listening device. If that were the case, Bluetooths would fit our ears better.

Excited as I was to get my first cell phone, I have come to hate the little beasties. They have come to rule our lives, and, frankly, I resent it. My life is fraught with communication. When I get up in the morning, the television comes on so I can hear the news and see if I need an alternate route to work because of traffic accidents.

...
One thing I absolutely refuse to do is talk on the telephone. I let the answering machine get it.
...

When I get to work, the desk phone, the computer and all of its email messages, and my clients yakking their personal woes fill my day. Eight hours of it. Without fail. Ring, ring, ring, ring. "You have 26 voice-mails...." "This fax is for you...You need to answer it yesterday."

When I get home, the TV is on for the news (again), to see what I missed while I was at work, and so that I don't miss

NCIS, Burn Notice, or *White Collar.* My home phone is sitting there like a silent vulture, just waiting for me to get settled down in my favorite chair, with whatever pastime I'm going to engage in (laptop or DSL for a video game or my crochet or jewelry-making equipment, if that's what strikes my fancy at the time) because I find it impossible to sit still and just watch TV. I'm so keyed up from the stresses of the day that I have to be doing something, anything. But the one thing I absolutely refuse to do—refuse, I say!—is talk on the telephone. I do that enough during the day, dammit! So, that's exactly when the silent vulture chooses to come alive. I won't take it. I let the answering machine get it.

At this point, we have reached the crux of the problem. I'm not the only one who lets the answering machine become our only representative to the world at large, the receptionist to take the messages so we can pick and choose which issues we want to deal with and which ones we're going to avoid until they go away all by themselves.

> ...
> **My answering machine is civilized. Is yours?**
> ...

My answering machine is civilized. Is yours? My answering machine says something standard, like "You've reached 999-9999. I can't take your call right now, but if you'll leave your name, number, and a brief message, I'll get back to you as soon as possible. Thanks for calling and have a good day." There is nothing offensive in this. It's bland, it's white bread, it's downright corporate.

In my current job with the government, I have to place calls to lots of clients. The messages I reach at the other end of my phone are very frequently shocking, to say the least. I have reached messages that were so sloppily recorded that they were unintelligible. I had no idea if I had reached the correct person or not. I have listened to some of the most riveting rap music I have ever heard, with truly romantic lyrics like "Slap the bitch! Hit that bitch!" And that's the tame stuff! I've listened to outright pornographic recordings that, I'm sure, the recording artist who put it together thought to be works of true art.

> ...
> **Clean up your answering machine and your cell phone messages. The messages I hear are frequently shocking, to say the least.**
> ...

It's one thing to express yourself. I think our Constitution allows us the right to do that. The problem is, sometimes you just have to choose between expressing yourself and actually getting a job. If a representative from X Company needs to call you to set up an interview and hears your answering machine going on and on musically about how much you like big butts, the chances are good your big butt is going to be unemployed a little longer!

Clean up your answering machine and your cell phone message, too, if you list that as a phone number you can be reached at. Hiring managers rarely exhibit a sense of humor.

9

That Ugly Application

Where the Rubber Meets the Road – What You Need to Know About Paper and Online Applications

You probably thought that filling out a job application would be enough to get you hired. As I've already said, ha-ha-ha!!! That's so funny because (1) paper applications exist only in magical forests now or in towns populated with fewer than 42 people, and (2) online applications fall under the malevolent scrutiny of evil computers that already hate you. Applications are tricky, and they are only one component of the perfect resume + appropriate cover letter + flawless application equation.

Let's talk about both kinds of applications. (Long, detailed chapter alert! This is going to take a while, so if you didn't get a sandwich back when you got the Coke for the resume chapter, go do that now. Okay. Good. Let's get on with it.)

Companies still utilizing paper applications are already pretty much suspect to me. To me, it sig-

> ...
> Companies still utilizing paper applications are already pretty much suspect to me.
> ...

nifies that they're very small companies, lacking computer savvy or access to people who can manage a database, or they're very lazy and don't want to invest in the resources it would take to turn their business into an Internet-age venture. Maybe it's not that they're lazy, but that they lack the money to get the equipment, perform the software engineering and web design necessary to create the web page and online application tools they need. If that's the case, run like the devil because if that's true, your paycheck may be in danger of bouncing if you go to work for them.

Paper applications are vanishing along with the trees cut down to make those paper applications. We're all supposed to be living in a web-based world now, where all of our data is stored somewhere in cyberspace, a mystical place that contains every bit of information about you as a person, a citizen, an employee, a husband and father, a wife and mother, a compulsive gambler, a Mason or anything else you may be in life. Cyberspace is a frightening place that can only be approached through a computer keyboard and you will have to approach it cautiously, make friends with it, and then share your deepest, darkest secrets with it…in an Online Application.

Online Applications ask the same questions that old-style paper applications ask. They just do it in a much more intimidating way because we all know that computers know everything and they will know instinctively if you're lying, like paper applications never could. Computers are linked with every other computer in the world, so if you stretch the truth, leave out an important bit of information, or list anything at all that is suspect, the computer will alert its other computer friends and suddenly your whole life will flash before their little silicon eyes and expose you for who and what you are: Unworthy.

More important than that, an application is a legal document. Even though there's no little balding man standing beside you while you're filling it out, dolefully intoning "Do you solemnly swear that what you are about to enter on this keyboard is the truth, the whole truth, and nothing but the truth, so help you, Bill Gates?," he is there in spirit. If you deliberately list incorrect information on an application, and then the company hires you and subsequently finds out about those lies, you are toast! I say this in the kindest way, but it's true. If you falsify employment information on a job application, it's almost as bad as trying to claim the family pot-belly pig as a dependent on your income tax. The government has no

> ...
> **An application is a legal document. If you deliberately list incorrect information you are toast!**
> ...

sense of humor and neither do corporations. They will first fire you, then they will blackball you, which will make it difficult to ever get another job, with or without lying.

Companies actually do spend the money these days on investigative services to check out the backgrounds of potential employees. They don't want to spend the money for training an employee (sometimes a considerable amount of time and money are involved) only to find something so unsavory in that person's past that all of those resources were wasted. It's more than just for the sake of corporate image. As with most issues in the corporate world, it's about the bottom line and expediency. Many companies will go ahead and hire a potential employee who shows real promise just to get them on board and then conduct the background check, hoping for the best. Sometimes that pans out, sometimes it doesn't.

Let's talk specifically about what you can expect to find on an application. Have you seen one recently? Since, as I said earlier, paper applications pretty much went out with internal combustion engines (oh, you don't plug your car into an electrical outlet yet?), we're going to look mostly at applications of the online variety.

Most online applications will ask you first for the obvious information: Your last name, first name, and middle initial; the date of the application (this is a test, do you know what the date is?); your home address (street address, city, state, Zip code); home and cell telephone numbers; and your Social Security number (although there is a lot of movement afoot to make it illegal to have the Social Security number on an application).

They're going to want to know what days and hours you would like to work, how much you would like to get paid, and if you or any of your immediate family have ever been employed by that particular company in the past. If you answer "Yes" to this, they're going to want to know the location of your assignment and the dates you were there. Then they're going to go straight to HR and find out if there is a DNR ("Do Not Re-hire") designation on your file.

They're going to want to know if you are currently employed and if they can contact your present employer. What to do, what to do? If you are still employed and you say "Yes," they can contact your current employer, you run the risk of alerting your current boss that you're looking elsewhere, anywhere elsewhere, for a better job, and then they might resent this and take it out on you for the remainder of your employment life with them, which is probably another two weeks. If you say no, they can't contact your present employer, you're raising a red flag that says, "I'm desperate to get away from that miserable armpit-of-the-universe company that I work for before it sucks the life out of me, but if you call them they'll kill me, they'll kill my family, they'll kill my family dog! Please, just hire me already!!!"

They'll ask if you are a citizen of the United States or about your Green Card, if you aren't. They'll ask about all of the other aliases you may have used, such as a maiden name (for women), but not your nickname from the bowling alley.

They will ask—it's getting ugly now—if you've ever been terminated from a job. Let's talk about "terminated." That means "fired." The word "separated" also means "fired." The words "Asked to Resign" mean "fired." The word "downsized" means "laid off." Don't get these mixed up. The word "ever" means since you emerged from the womb. If you answer "Yes" to this question, you have to provide details. How's your dancing? You're going to have to do a tap dance worthy of "Dancing With The Stars" to get around that question. Be as honest as you can be, but don't give too much detail either. Whatever you do, if this has actually happened to you, don't lie about it. If your termination included something really juicy that will probably knock you out of the running anyway, write "Will discuss in person" or "Will discuss in interview." Then, if you get the interview, you can finesse the conversation in such a way that you can come across in the best light. (This may take some practice, and we'll talk more about this in Chapter 11.)

> ...
> **Be as honest as you can be, but don't give too much detail either. Whatever you do, don't lie about it.**
> ...

They're going to ask you if you have ever been convicted of or pleaded guilty or "no contest" to any violation of the law other than a minor traffic violation. Because I'm devoting an entire chapter to ex-offenders, I'm going to table this topic for now and take it up again in Chapter 10. (Please read it, it's a good one!)

You're going to be asked to list your work history, going back (usually) seven to 10 years. It is not uncommon to be asked to list periods of unemployment just as if they were companies where you had worked in order to fill in the time gaps in your work history. The same is true of military service or incarceration.

For each employer, you will need to provide the company's name, address, and phone number; your job title there; your starting and ending salaries; the starting and ending dates of your employment; your supervisor's name; your reason for leaving; and a short description of your job duties there. You can't get away with not listing employment dates here. Failure to disclose information is the same as giving false information, and, remember, this is a **legal document**. It's not your resume, which is, after all, a marketing tool.

The job application is where the rubber meets the road, for all of you baby boomers who remember your old tire commercials. The information you provide here—or fail to provide—can make or break you. My favorite "Reason for Leaving" is "Changed corporate goals resulting in downsizing," or "Inappropriate job fit resulting in resignation (or termination)." You'll have to discuss what this actually means in the interview, but if you use either of these explanations, you at least stand a chance of getting the interview.

You will be asked to provide your educational accomplishments. That may be your high school diploma or a GED, but it could also include college degrees and certifications attained by going to a vocational/technical school. If you are still in college but haven't graduated yet, you can enter "College coursework in <u>your discipline here</u>, totaling <u>X-number</u> credit hours," then list the college by name, along with its city and state.

The application may or may not have an area that lists all kinds of equipment or machinery that you might be able to operate, and they almost certainly will ask you what kind of computer programs you can operate. Don't list programs you may have heard of but don't really know how to use. If you mark "Word" on that application, the company has a right to expect you to be able to produce documents utilizing Word for Windows.

> ...
> **Don't list programs you may have heard of but don't really know how to use.**
> ...

The application will almost always list boxes for you to enter contact information for at least three personal references. They are going to ask for the person's name, address, phone number, as well as how long you have known them and in what capacity? Are you listing your relatives or your drinking buddies? Provide these references carefully, and, for God's sake, talk it over with the people you choose, to give them a thumbs-up that they might be receiving an inquiry from a potential employer. I'll never forget giving a glowing reference for my sister, only to let it slip that we were related. She had told them that I was a former client of hers, not her sister. I felt like a complete idiot. I've never provided a telephone reference for anybody since that time.

The application will usually have boxes to upload your resume and your cover letter, both of which we've already talked about. If there is a box in the application for a cover letter, it is **not** optional. They expect you to attach one. Make sure you have spell-checked both of these documents before you hit that "Send" key.

There will no doubt be some kind of Records Release form on or attached to the application. It isn't legal these days for anyone to obtain personal information about anyone without due process[8], so you will have to sign and date a Consent to Release Form that allows companies to sic those investigators onto the background check that will expose any reasons there may be out there for them to not hire you.

These are the core areas that will almost assuredly appear in most online applications. Another thing that is cropping up is a series of behavioral questions at the end of the application, placed there to help weed out applicants who don't have the requisite experience in certain situations.

For instance, you may be asked to describe a circumstance where you couldn't meet a deadline and to explain how you handled that. Or you may be asked to explain your feelings about a situation where you were the only team member wanting to go home on time when the rest of your co-workers wanted to work overtime to complete an overdue project.

These are touchy-feely questions that are expected to be difficult to answer and are supposed to reveal Deep, Dark Secrets about personality. I give my clients copies of a list of one hundred potential interview questions so they can prepare for any of these to be thrown at them in an interview. These same questions are finding their way onto online applications, so it's more important than ever to practice your answers. This list is included here, and, I promise you, I didn't write the list. These are real questions that have been asked by real interviewers. Take the list, close your eyes, poke that finger down there on the list, then quickly answer the question. Do this until no question can possibly throw you now. You'll be glad you took the time.

Of course, not all applications are exactly like this, but these are the basics. Some applications may delve deeper into diplomatically worded questions about whether you have been criticized in the past year (or whatever time period they choose) for drinking or using drugs. This is a legal way for them to find out if you're a lush or a user without coming out and directly asking you if you are one. Be careful. Read these questions several times before answering them.

Remember, applications are legal documents! Let me say that again, **legal documents**! What that means is, you're going to have to live with this as your Permanent Record for however long you are at that company, if they hire you, and any information you provide in that application can and will be used against you if they need it. Beware! **Really**, be careful.

10

Now Let's Talk About That Felony Conviction of Yours

Stuff You Won't Get From Most Books Like This

It was on a particularly hot summer night, and you and a couple of your homies went to a bar to see if you could get a little sumpun-sumpun goin'. Your boys spot three really fine ladies at a table in the back and the math works, three of you, three of them, so you all go back and start putting your moves down. Your boys' ladies are laughing and flirting, but yours just sits there. Every time you try to start something up, she just turns the other way. Who do she think she be, anyway? She sittin' there with her funbags hangin' out and disrespecting you! Finally, all of you leave and you follow her home. She think she all that! You follow her to her apartment to show her who da man! Conviction: Rape.

* * *

It didn't seem like such a big deal. Nobody would ever miss the money. There was so much cash flowing into the organization, and your best friend was the office manager. She would make sure that nobody noticed while you cooked the books and arranged for amounts of cash to disappear, a little here and a little there. But it wasn't a little bit of cash, was it? It ended up amounting to thousands, and you and Grace split it evenly. But it was for a good cause. After all, you think, George is on dialysis now and the medical bills are rolling in so fast. You really need the money and neither of you is getting any younger. Conviction: Embezzlement.

* * *

The car belonged to a friend's dad, so your buddy said. You and a couple other kids went for a ride up on the bluff one evening after school, but Jake was driving just a little too fast and you got stopped by the police. As it turned out, the car was stolen, and Jake hadn't mentioned anything at all about the little plastic bag under the seat with the white powder in it. Conviction: Auto Theft and Narcotics Possession.

* * *

You came home after work one night, really beat. You expected to find dinner on the table, but what you found was your wife in bed with some guy you'd never seen before. You went out to the truck and took your rifle out of the rack. Conviction: Murder.

* * *

The food stamps got turned off because you didn't turn in your job search logs like you were supposed to. The kids are hungry, the utilities are off, and you just don't know what to do next. You can't go to your parents for money again. After all, they disapprove of everything you've ever done, including being with your baby-daddy and having those kids. You're on your own and desperate. Even though the baby-daddy is long gone, the nine-millimeter Glock he brought home one night is still in the hall closet. You get it and go down to the liquor store. Conviction: Armed Robbery.

* * *

The office party was really great this year! Man, the boss really went all out, with the food and the open bar! You and Jennifer ate a lot, drank a little, then headed home, but it had started raining while you were at the party. The oil was on the surface of the road and it was a little slick. Your head was just a little fuzzy and the headlights bothered your eyes. You were a little sleepy, too, to top it all off. The red light really didn't register on you and you went through it, plowing into the side of a passenger car and killing the driver. Your blood alcohol was .20. Conviction: Vehicular Manslaughter.

* * *

You've been out of work for two years now. The construction industry has been dead in your state for at least four years and things don't look like they're going to get any better. You've been divorced for five years and you keep trying to explain to the judge and your ex that it's not that you don't want to pay the child support, you just aren't working and you don't have the money. The judge keeps warning you to get a job and get caught up on those payments or else! How are you supposed to write a check when you have no money coming in to pay it with? Finally, the judge makes good on his threats. Conviction: Non-Payment of Child Support.

* * *

Some are accidents, some are acts of passion, and some are pre-meditated crimes. Regardless of which scenario you look at, all of these people share the same label now: Felon. What does that mean for their future? From an employment standpoint, it means they're probably screwed.

These people are actually the reason I'm writing this book. Through my years in workforce development, I've come to realize how few people really understand the processes in place to receive unemployment benefits or welfare, and fewer still have any idea how to bounce back once they're on unemployment. Take the basic fact of unemployment and add to it the barrier of a felony conviction and you have the most serious challenge a person could face in becoming success-fully employed ever again. Depending upon the nature of the conviction, they may or may not be employable at all.

I became interested in working with felons when I came to see what kind of people were becoming felons these days. Kids who never quite got the message that all it takes is one little mistake to destroy your entire life. Seemingly well-adjusted adults who have a major life event that sends them into an emotional spi-ral, then on to an impulsive, violent act, which, in turn, sends them to prison. Men (or women) who were the breadwinners for their families before divorce crops up and leaves them with the responsibility for child support they can't pay due to unemployment or just being up to their ears in debt.

> ...
> **It takes one little mistake to destroy your entire life.**
> ...

We're seeing a new kind of criminal these days. People like those above, who don't really seem to fit in with the hard-boiled criminals of the past who chose and stalked their vic-tims or carefully planned out their crime of choice. The pris-ons are full of these new convicts, side by side with rapists and drug dealers and traffickers in human slavery. The times we live in are showing our stress levels in ways that we, the taxpayers, are paying for big time. There needs to be a ma-jor overhaul of our criminal justice system, or we're going to need to dedicate a single state to turn into a federal prison, like they did in the movie "Escape From New York."

I trained to become an Offender Workforce Develop-ment Specialist so that I could use the skills that I already possessed, along with the newest theories put forth by the U.S. Department of Justice, in an effort to help ex-offenders re-establish themselves in society and keep from having to return to prison. It isn't easy work. The biggest challenge we face in this field is the lack of jobs in general. With the really awful job market that makes it nigh unto impossible for trained, educated, experienced adults to find decent, stable jobs, let alone careers, it is an impossibility of astronomical proportions for someone with major barriers like a felony conviction to find work worth doing, work that can sustain not only an individual but the family they may be returning to and which is now depending upon this person to support them. Everything I've been saying in this book about changes that have to be made to adjust to the new economy is magnified a thousand-fold for such individuals.

> ...
> **The biggest challenge we face in this field is the lack of jobs in general.**
> ...

The first challenge for the ex-offender in the job search arena is the obvious obstacle of the application. All job applications have some kind of carefully worded question that asks if the applicant has been convicted of any violation of the law more serious than a minor traffic infraction. Some of these ask if you have "ever" been convicted; others state specific time frames, such as in the last seven or four years. This becomes tricky. If a felon was released last week from prison, after serving seven years, then fills out an application that asks if in the last four years he had been convicted of a felony, the answer is "No." That sounds quite promising and is, technically, correct. However, when the company does a background check and discovers the felony, it's not really going to matter if it occurred in the last four or 40 years. They're not going to want to hire him.

The question on the application about the felony conviction **must** be answered. An application is, as I said, a legal document, and you just can't dodge that old technicality. If you leave the question blank, some companies will assume the worst and just throw the application out. If you answer "No," when the answer is really "Yes," you will be found out when the background check comes back. If you answer "Yes," you'll be expected to provide details of that conviction right there on the application, to be viewed by one person after the other in the Human Resources office, and for all the secretaries to discuss over their Subway sandwiches at lunch. If you should get the job, you're always going to wonder how many people know all the details of your sordid history.

> ...
> **The question on the application about the felony conviction must be answered.**
> ...

There is another way. You will first write in the blank provided "Will discuss in the interview," and then you will need to attach a "Letter of Explanation." Type out the letter, personalized for the company you're applying to, according to the form letter in Appendix E (page 132), seal it in a plain envelope, and staple it to the application. This is necessary to maintain your privacy. There's no guarantee that you'll still be considered, but at least you have a chance.

I recommend that job seekers do the same thing if they're filling out an online application. The difference is, the Letter of Explanation becomes your cover letter. There's no way to keep Sally Jo in HR from seeing your letter when the downloaded application finds its way to her desk, but it's important to get the details of the conviction out there in the open up-front, and actually entering those details into the very small space provided for the conviction details on the application doesn't allow for the words of persuasion needed to overcome objections. On that online application, where the question appears, "How you ever been convicted of a felony?" you will simply write, "See cover letter."

Ex-offender resumes must be tailored to raise no flags when it comes to time-period gaps in their work histories from their period(s) of incarceration, or they won't stand a chance of getting an interview. Felons are going to need to use the functional-style resume, of course, and will need to really beef up the skills section to show abilities because, obviously, their actual employment history is going to come up short. Employment periods during incarceration—such as being employed in a prison manufacturing facility—can be counted toward employment and that helps a lot to fill in time periods.

> ...
> **A job seeker needs to write their own 30-Second Commercial and memorize it.**
> ...

Remember, the application doesn't get you hired. The resume doesn't get you hired, it only gets you an interview. You get you hired, and you do it in the interview. The biggest challenge of all is going to be if, and when, the felon gets that interview. He is going to have to handle it with a very special two-pronged approach. The first part is what we call the "30-Second Commercial" and it's quite frankly stolen from the corporate world. I recommend this for all job seekers, but it's vitally important for ex-offenders to master.

In the world of big business, you meet hundreds of movers and shakers, decision-makers who can, with a word, make or break the career of anyone. An accidental encounter in an elevator can be the single most important contact in a job seeker's life. I encountered Donald Trump once, in an elevator. Had I known then what I know now, I might have been able to make an impression on him and be writing for his enterprises today. Oh, well, water under the bridge....

What we know is that an individual has only 30 seconds to make a good impression on a stranger. For this reason, a job seeker needs to write their own 30-Second Commercial and memorize it. I tell them to introduce themselves to their refrigerator, their hall closet door, their dog, their bathroom mirror, practicing it over and over again until it's second nature and they can say it in their sleep.

I learned this about 10 years ago when I was working at that big card company and encountered the occasional celebrity and other people who thought they were. It was a commonly used tool for networking at the time, and it's become even more important now, as our world speeds up and our opportunities to meet decision-makers become fewer.

My 30-Second Commercial might sound something like this: "Hi, I'm Cheryl. I'm a FlippityFloppityWhatever, working for the state. I've been there about seven years now, but it's just been recently that I've started working with ex-offenders and put together my own workshop. It's going great, attendance is good, and it shows real promise."

Okay, I haven't exactly recited my entire resume, but in 30 seconds or less you've learned who I am, where I work, how long I've been there, what I'm doing right now, and how I feel about it. That's a lot of information to communicate in 30 seconds. If you were a hiring manager, would you remember me?

This crazy little exercise serves two purposes. First, it's a way to make contact with people when you only have a short time to make an impression. Second, you're going to have to go to a job interview sometime, and this is going to come into play then. The first thing interviewers say to job applicants is "Tell me something about yourself." This is when you rattle off that 30-Second Commercial that you've practiced so well. After you've done that, sit there and **shut up**! Wait out the silence until the interviewer asks, "Could you tell me a little more about yourself?" Then the felon is going to launch into the "Incarceration Speech."

> ...
> **Employers have the right to know about the felony conviction.**
> ...

The second prong of the two-pronged approach to the interview for ex-offenders is what I was taught was the "Three R's" but which I have adjusted to be the "Four R's" and what is also known as the "Incarceration Speech."

Employers have the right to know about the felony conviction. In many cases, it's going to determine if a convict can legally perform the kind of work the company wants him to do. Sometimes it's simply a matter of whether their insurance company will allow a felon to serve in a certain capacity. Either way, the company has the right to know about that conviction. At the same time, a felon doesn't want to scare the company and definitely wants to emphasize the fact that all of that bad history is just that: history. It's in the past. They don't need to worry about it anymore.

Now, I've been told that employers are like most people, that they are inherently forgiving and want to see people bounce back from adversity. I'm not sure what universe this is in, because it sure isn't that way in my neighborhood. In the country I live in, which was historically, by the way, based on the concept that a person was innocent until proven guilty, I find that it's quite the other way around. An individual is guilty until proven innocent. I don't care what the law says. What I see demonstrated again and again and played out in the media for all to see are the results of backroom courthouse deals and plea bargains and the modern Golden Rule: He who has the gold, rules. We live more and more in a world of unforgiveness, non-forgetfulness, and unwillingness to lend a hand to the less fortunate. If a person makes a mistake in this harshly critical world, they have forfeited their right to live a normal life, ever again. There are no second acts in this new world.

> ...
> **The felon needs to use the "Four R's": Right to Know, Responsibility, Regret, and Redemption.**
> ...

However, for what it's worth, a felon may find a soft heart or a person willing to be the exception, who will give them a chance to prove himself or herself. In order to find that out, the felon needs to use the "Four R's":

1. **Right to Know**—The employer has a right to know about the conviction (what it was and when it happened).

2. **Responsibility**—The employer wants to hear that the felon can man-up and take responsibility for his own actions. God didn't make him commit the crime, his friends didn't make him do it, he himself made his choices, including whatever it was that sent him to prison.

3. **Regret**—The employer wants to hear genuine regret for the pain and suffering caused to the felon's family,

friends, and anyone involved in the crime, including his victim's family.

4. **Redemption**—The employer wants to hear positive ways the felon has changed his life for the better, what he has learned about himself and his decisions, and he wants to hear that he has grown and moved on in his life.

This would sound something like this in an interview:

Employer: "I see that you've marked that you have been convicted of a felony. Can you tell me something about that?"

Felon: "Yes, and thank you for giving me the opportunity to discuss this with you. I understand that you would have reservations about hiring someone like me, but you do have a right to know what happened and I want to tell you about it. Some years ago, I was involved with a group of friends, and together, we decided to steal a car and rob a convenience store. I don't blame my friends. I was young and hot-headed and it seemed like a good idea at the time. We were apprehended, convicted, and I served my time. While I was incarcerated, I took a lot of classes that let me explore why I would do such a thing, and I've learned a lot about myself. Because of that, I know I can state that nothing like that will ever happen again. I've become better at interacting with a variety of people and handling stressful situations. I took vocational courses to improve my job skills. As you know, I'm a [insert your profession or trade here], and I'm really good at it. If you'll give me a chance to prove myself, I'm sure you'll see that no one will work harder to help your company succeed and grow."

This is called the "Incarceration Speech." It is vital that every felon have one, have it practiced, and be able to deliver it smoothly. When a felon first uses the 30-Second Commercial and then follows it up by the Incarceration Speech, all of the ugly stuff is out there on the table at the very beginning of an interview. There are basically no surprises after this point.

If, after giving the 30-Second Commercial and the Incarceration Speech the interviewer still wants more details about the conviction, the appropriate answer is something like, "You know, that happened so long ago that I don't even think about it anymore. That's not who I am now. I'd like to discuss what I can offer your company." If they're still plumbing for details, it's out of pure curiosity and they probably have decided not to hire a felon anyway.

> ...
> **The federal bonding program, is offered by the federal government and covers the company for any loss it may incur by hiring the individual.**
> ...

If the interviewer continues to display interest in the ex-offender, he should bring up additional reasons why it is in the company's interest to hire him. There is the **federal bonding program**, whereby an insurance policy is offered by the federal government and covers the company for any loss it may incur by hiring the individual. It is at no cost to the company, and should equipment go missing or some other loss occurs, even if the ex-offender himself is not implicated, the policy will pay off, no questions asked.

There is also the **Work Opportunity Tax Credit** that offers a tax credit to anyone hiring an ex-offender. The hiring company fills out the appropriate forms and submits them to their state, and that company is issued a tax credit, based on the ex-offender's salary, for a period of the first year of their employment. It's a nice little incentive to give the felon a chance to prove his or her ability to re-enter the work world and make a meaningful contribution to the company.

> ...
> **The Work Opportunity Tax Credit offers a tax credit to anyone hiring an ex-offender.**
> ...

In the world of ex-offender employment, the biggest hurdles are faced by those convicted of three types of crime:

- Assault
- Murder
- Sex Crimes

Individuals with these raps hanging over them are going to have to face the wrath of the communities they choose to settle down in, the legal requirements of registering with offender websites, and with the specters of their pasts coloring every single relationship, whether personal or professional. Obviously, the most difficult of these three convictions to bounce back from is a conviction of sex crimes. Assault and murder can be argued to be crimes of passion, quite frequently, but there can be no real explanation of sex crimes as being anything other than pre-meditated. Such a job seeker will need to work a little harder and prepare a little more extensively before speaking with anyone in a job interview. Individuals convicted of sex crimes will have to prepare a "Rehabilitation Portfolio."

A Rehabilitation Portfolio is a folder that collects in one place all of the documents and letters that can be obtained from therapists, counselors, doctors, and any mental health professionals willing to provide documentation that states that the individual has been treated and counseled and is no longer liable to commit sex crimes. This portfolio can contain certificates or reports from classes or sessions the individual has participated in that can indicate progress made toward rehabilitation. It is compiled in an effort to show basic, measurable change in the personality and behavior of the ex-offender. It needs to be taken with the individual to a job interview and be presented if the question of rehabilitation is brought up. It may sway the interviewer in favor of giving the ex-offender a chance.

> ...
> **For ex-offenders, there are no easy fixes. They have to work harder to make themselves attractive job candidates.**
> ...

For ex-offenders, there are no easy fixes. They have to work harder to make themselves attractive job candidates. Many companies have corporate policies that won't allow them to hire felons. As I understand it, that is being considered in our country's high courts right now in an effort to label companies' refusals to hire ex-offenders as discrimination. No one can predict which way this argument will go in the future.

What we can predict is what will happen if ex-offenders can't find work. Put yourself in this position: You've been convicted of a crime, you've served your sentence, and now you can't get a job. You have 30 days to find work or go back to jail. Now answer this question: If you can't find a legitimate job, what do you do? Come on, you know the answer to this. There are two possibilities. You go ahead and turn yourself in and reclaim your prison jumpsuit, or you go back to work in the only way you know how to make a living. If you stole, you'll steal again. If you sold drugs, you'll be contacting your supplier any day now.

Who is going to reap the rewards of preventing felons from finding gainful employment? The answer is: Nobody. The community is victimized. The felon goes back to jail. The felon's family has to depend upon public assistance. Taxpayers have to support another occupant of an already-crowded prison system. Nobody wins.

If it's going to take legislation to promote second-chance opportunities, then so be it. We've got to help ex-offenders become productive citizens again, and there just isn't any way around it. Companies don't have to like it. The public doesn't have to like it, but they sure have to think about it, because offenders are picking up your trash on trash trucks, they're sacking your groceries, and they're living in your neighborhoods. Get over it, people.

11

So You Landed an Interview. Now What?

Take Out That Nose Ring, Cover Up That Gang Tattoo, and, for God's Sake, Pull Up Those Pants!

Back in junior high school—middle school to anyone younger than me; *you* know who you are—I wore a short black skirt to school. Now, I need to say that this skirt was short. It was brief in length. It was very non-long. That was when the "mini-skirt" had just made its debut. I think it was about six inches long. Well, six inches *short*. I just need to make that very clear. I paired it with a black and gold sweater that fit snuggly in the frontal, chestish area. I thought it looked "fab" as we said then because my generation had just invented The Beatles and we were all pretending to be British.

I wore it to school. I got sent to the principal's office because that was the era when teachers—whether they were nuns or not—measured the length of girls' skirts with a ruler. My mother was called and she came to school to see what the big beef was about. When she got there, she laughed and laughed. Not because of how I looked, but because the sweater was hers and she had no idea I had "borrowed" it.

That wasn't the reaction the school staff had in mind. They felt that I deserved a serious reprimand for flaunting such individuality in the face of their well-ingrained regulations for proper female attire. Everybody knew that "proper" female students wore skirts that didn't go above the knee, downplayed their chest expansions (if they were in any way showing at that age), and didn't wear makeup or "tease" their hair. Which is exactly why I did all of those things. I was a rebel, seriously expressing my own character and tastes. My mother sided with me, told off the school people, and bought me another short skirt and a tight sweater of my own, so I would leave hers alone. What's all this got to do with you getting an interview? Don't rush me, I'm getting to that!

> **...**
> **Landing a job is about making choices. You're going to need to look right for the job, act appropriately in the interview, and give the interviewers the answers that will satisfy them.**
> **...**

I went on to high school and heard about how tough the world was and the fact that I would have to conform to certain standards if I wanted to "make it" in the world and be rewarded with an impressive amount of currency for my conformity to "the system." I caved, as most people of my generation did, except for the ones who went to Canada. I grew up, became corporate, and cashed my paychecks. Yum! Good paychecks!

You should sort of have an idea of where this is headed by now. Landing a job is about making choices. You're going to need to look right for the job, act appropriately in the interview, and give the interviewers the answers that will satisfy them that you are a good fit for their organization. You're going to have to put your personality back in the closet and choose to be corporate if you're going to succeed. I had to do it; so do you.

Appearance

I don't want to get ethnic here, because, in truth, this isn't even about ethnicity. I've seen waist bands hugging the knees of young black, Hispanic, white, and Asian guys. It's not about their ethnic group—let's face it, it's about style. The fact does remain, however, that, if you want to get a job, you're going to have to make a choice between wearing your nose ring and all of those eyebrow-, lip-, and excessive ear-piercings, or showing the tattoos that start on your shoulder and run all the way to the tips of your fingers, or wearing the pants-waistband-around-the-knees pants with the tidy whities sticking out for about six inches at the top, and getting that job. Choices.

If you really are all of your piercings, the tattoos, and low-riding pants and you just can't bear to part with them or hide them, then you're going to have to get a grip on a very simple fact: No one is going to hire you. Nobody. I'm not even sure the local crack dealer will hire you to manage distribution because being low-key and under-the-radar is essential to not getting busted. The easiest way in the world to get nailed by the DEA is to be represented by someone looking like a gang-banger.

> ...
> **Just look nice. You know what nice is. Something your grandmother could see you in.**
> ...

And ladies, *ladies*…You are not exempt from the rules of modern attire. I know, style is style, baby, but please, please don't wear your underwear on the outside for a job interview. Put the funbags back where they belong for the daylight hours, try to take notice of what's currently considered a proper corporate look and try to emulate it as much as possible. I don't mean you have to go out and pop for a really expensive suit or Hermes scarf or wear Jimmy Choo shoes or whatever they're pushing on TV shows these days. Just look nice. You know what *nice* is. Something your grandmother could see you in without trying to hide from being identified as your blood relation.

It's very simple, really. Decide which is more important to you: (1) Maintaining your individuality by refusing to take the piercings out, refusing to wear long-sleeve shirts to cover the tattoos, refusing to buy a belt to keep the pants up so you don't have to go around with your hand on your handle, or dressing like a lady of the night, or (2) Realizing the requirements and the necessary "uniform" of the employment market and come to grips with the fact that you have to look like everybody else or you won't stand a chance at landing a job.

> ...
> **Guys, there's one requirement you must provide for your interview wardrobe: a necktie. Ladies, look like ladies.**
> ...

Would I have followed this advice had I heard it when I was young? Well, not at 13, but by 18 I was getting the idea and by 20 I had sold out. It was in my early 20s that I became totally aware of who was succeeding and who wasn't, and I decided that bucking the system wasn't as important as earning the bucks to buy any kind of clothes I wanted to wear off-duty.

You, too, will have to decide. You're checking out your interview clothes now, aren't you? Guys, if you don't own a suit, you can get by with decent pants and a shirt, but there's one requirement you must provide for your interview wardrobe: a necktie. You can wear "business casual" and get away with it as long as your clothes are clean and you wear a necktie that blends well with the shirt you choose. If you don't know how to tie a tie, buy a clip-on. Ladies, look like *ladies*.

Cell Phones

Cell phone usage in this book is prohibited. Please turn your cell phones off or set them to vibrate. Thank you.

There are places in the world where cell phones are just considered obnoxious. You wouldn't take a call in the middle of a funeral, you shouldn't take calls during the church sermon, and it's never appropriate to be fiddling with the phone in a business meeting. I don't mean just answering the phone, I mean looking at it, reading your messages, texting. You should not be accessing the Internet on your phone, checking football scores, looking at pictures, or playing games. You will have all the time in the world to do that while you sit at home, unemployed, waiting for "The Bold and The Beautiful" to come on. If you land an interview, keep in mind the fact that this is the Ultimate Business Meeting. This can make or break your future. Treat it with the seriousness it deserves.

Attitude

You are meeting with someone who already has a job. They aren't losing anything if they don't hire you, they'll just go on to the next candidate. It is no big deal to an interviewer if you go in with a chip on your shoulder and express your dissatisfaction with their company, salary or benefits offered, or any other issues you might want to discuss. You are there as the supplicant. You are wanting to be hired. You have to display an appropriate attitude. You have to be courteous.

The two prevalent attitudes that hiring managers are seeing right now are equally bad when it comes to impressing an interviewer. The first one is typical of youth and the second of older adults.

Surly/Uncommunicative

Many young people approach job interviews with a sense of entitlement. They believe they should get the job just because they showed up for the interview. They slouch, they don't dress correctly, they don't exhibit basic manners, they don't speak well. I don't mean they have to be public speakers. I mean they need to know that if they are asked a question, they are expected to answer in a way that conveys information. "Yes" and "No" answers will not cut it. In an interview, a question is asked to determine the way the candidate thinks, reacts, and performs. The questions will sometimes be phrased to determine attention to detail and the ability to think on one's feet. Our young people just don't seem to get this. If you are a parent and have children nearing the age when they'll be getting a job, do them a favor and explain this to them. Then teach them how to properly shake hands. Both males and females need to learn this. In the business world, they'll be shaking hundreds of hands.

> ...
> **Many young people approach job interviews with a sense of entitlement.**
> ...

Desperate

This attitude is more endemic to our adult population. Because of the horrible job market and desperate economy we find ourselves in at this time, desperation prevails across the board among adult job seekers. "I can do anything." "I'll take anything." We know this is true, and it's understandable and a valid feeling. As adults, we know that we have families to support; we have obligations. We are responsible. We will do whatever it takes.

The problem with that is, when an employer senses desperation in a candidate, he thinks, "If I give this guy a job, he's just going to be here long enough to find something better and then he'll quit." That may well be true, but you just can't let that attitude come across in an interview. When you go into that office to discuss what skills you possess and how you can contribute to that company, the one thing on your mind should be to convince the interviewer that this job is the only job you will ever consider, but if you don't get it, that's okay, too; you'll just retire to your summer home and kick back for a while. Corny? Maybe. Necessary? Absolutely! Want the job, but don't want it too bad! Play just a little bit hard to get.

> ...
> **You have to practice your answers to interview questions.**
> ...

It sounds easy and yet I know it isn't. At home, you have to practice your answers to interview questions so you will know how you will answer the tough ones and deal with scenarios they can paint you into the corner with. That's why I've included in this book the list of "100 Potential Interview Questions," so you can practice, practice, practice…That's why agencies like Career Centers offer workshops in mock interviews and interviewing techniques.

It may feel silly doing a mock interview, but this is important, people! Too much is at stake to take it lightly. You're going to have to go to an interview prepared, mentally, physically, visually. Get plenty of sleep the night before. Try not to dwell on anything whatsoever that is negative. A positive frame of mind is so necessary. And, whatever you do, be PUNCTUAL!

> ...
> **There is no grace period for showing up, either to an interview or to work.**
> ...

For meetings in my office, the common denominator between my young and old clients is a basic inability to tell time. If a meeting is set for 8:00am, they may show up somewhere around 8:30am. In the business world, this is suicide. If you show up for a job interview a half hour late, you're telling the employer that you'll show up for work late. Since attendance is one of the few legal reasons a company can use to fire an employee now, this is really a big deal. There is no grace period for showing up, either to an interview or to work. If you're due to time in at 9:00, that means 9:00, not 9:01. Get used to it. It shows work ethic. Get one!

If you read the previous chapter about ex-offenders, you already know what I wrote about the 30-Second Commercial, (If you didn't, go back and read it. It's important!) Interviewers are trained to conduct interviews–no surprise there. They are supposed to ask certain questions, and usually in a specific order.

The most common first question in an interview isn't actually a question at all. It's "Tell me something about yourself." If you have written, practiced, and mastered your 30-Second

Commercial, this is an ideal way to begin your interview. Your 30-Second Commercial is going to showcase the thing about your professional accomplishments or your favorite job that you are most proud of. It isn't, as I've said before, a recitation of your resume. The interviewer has that in front of him or her. It's a way to launch into your discussion of your qualifications, but it's a hook to grab their interest. Deliver the 30-Second Commercial and then shut up! Yes, *shut up*!

The object of that particular "question" is to throw you off-balance. You enter an interview expecting to be asked a specific question, not to deliver an essay. If the interviewer can throw you off-balance, you will start to babble. At least I know that I have. If you babble, you're going to provide all kinds of information that the interviewer can't legally ask you. You may disclose your age, the fact that you have children at home, the fact that you were fired with prejudice from your last job, all kinds of juicy material that the interviewer can now go to work on, to find out other information they can use to disqualify you. **Don't** give it to them. Deliver the 30-Second Commercial then. shut up and wait for a specific question.

> ...
> **Remember to keep the discussion centered on the work world. Keep on-topic and discuss your skills.**
> ...

They may ask for more details, in which case you should be prepared to tell them what you can offer their company. Remember to keep the discussion centered on the **work world**. This is not the place to discuss your children, your marriage, your opinions. Keep on-topic and discuss your skills.

Other questions you will almost certainly be asked include "Tell me about your strengths," followed by its flip-side, "Tell me about your weaknesses". Your strengths shouldn't be hard to discuss. Your weaknesses are another matter. You need to take something that actually sounds like a weakness, but flip it so that it ends up seeming like a positive thing. For instance, when asked what one of my weaknesses is, I go with something like, "I have a tendency to go beyond the scope of my job and take on more work than I'm supposed to do. My co-workers take exception to that sometimes because it raises the bar and they think they'll have to take on more work as well." From the standpoint of an employer, that's probably not such a bad thing. Try to be honest, but not too honest. You can talk yourself right out of a job that way.

> ...
> **Try to be honest, but not too honest. You can talk yourself right out of a job that way.**
> ...

12

Thank-You Letters?

No Flowers, No Candy, No Crap

The very first thing you do after leaving the office of the interview is go home, sit down at your computer, and type out a simple, heart-felt thank-you letter.

Rule-of-thumb used to be that the letter should be hand-written, but we all have computers now, and, frankly, your handwriting isn't that great, so use your computer, plain white paper, and don't get too cutesy about the whole thing. Some people like to send greeting cards. Greeting card companies want you to send greeting cards. Don't bother. What that says is it's easier for you to sign your name to a card with a sentiment on it that you, yourself, weren't smart enough to write than for you to sit down and put a few simple thoughts about the meeting on paper. Type the letter.

> ...
> **Use your computer, plain white paper, and don't get too cutesy about the whole thing.**
> ...

You can find samples of thank-you letters all over the place, in books on resumes in the library and even online by going to www.google.com and typing in the search bar: **Thank you letter template**. Then choose the template for a job interview. The main things to remember are two: (1) Keep it simple, and (2) Do it! Do it right away! Don't put it off, because if you do, you'll never get around to writing and sending it, and, if you don't, you've just canceled out the possibility of you getting that job. HR people eat up thank-you letters. They live on that stuff. A thank-you letter is a simple thing. It looks something like this:

Today's Date

Name of Interviewer
Company
Address
City, State, ZIP

Dear Ms. Whatever:

I just wanted to drop you a note to let you know that I really appreciated you taking the time to talk to me today about the _____ job opening that you currently have at _____ Company.

As you'll recall, I have ____ years experience in the field. I'm sure I could make a significant contribution and be a real asset to your company. Thanks for your consideration.

Sincerely,

 [sign your name in longhand here]

Janice Jobseeker
Address
City, State, ZIP
Phone number(s)
Email address

Thank-you letters are a common courtesy. Male HR representatives may not think quite as much of it if you fail to write one and send it to them, but, trust me on this, a female HR person will never forgive nor forget! It's like a date. There are certain rules governing your conduct, and if you fail to follow through on this one, you have ended the relationship.

Flowers and candy just don't work. They're overkill. I only mention them because I know of someone who swears by them. The fact that that individual hasn't been gainfully employed on a regular basis sort of makes me doubt the wisdom of his advice, but he does seem to do well with his lady friends, most of whom, ironically, seem to be HR employees.

> ...
> **Send the thank-you letter promptly. Then sit back and wait.**
> ...

Send the thank-you letter promptly. Write it, spell-check it, stamp it (this is important), and mail it. Then sit back and wait. Better still, just assume that your contact with that company is now over, and move on to the next phase of your job search, starting over from Square One to contact another potential employer. So: Write letter, send letter, let it go, period.

13

Follow-Up

The Difference Between Keeping in Touch and Stalking

"Don't call us; we'll call you."
"We'll let you know if we're interested."
"This isn't a bus station. Don't make us call Security."
"Security!!!!"

Once you've done everything you could do, the hardest part has arrived: The Wait. We are creatures of action. It isn't in our nature to sit back and wait. We want to Make Something Happen. We want to Get On With Our Lives. And it's just damned rude of them to keep you dangling like that! They know if they're going to hire you or not, don't they? Maybe yes, maybe no, but you're sure not going to find out right away. Let me tell you about a weird little job-seeker ritual I was required to participate in at a company where I ended up working for 20 years.

I had left a life in one field and wasn't sure what I wanted to do next with my life or where I would end up doing it. I thought about returning to California but wasn't sure I could make it out there on my own. I needed a summer job to buy me some time until I could sort things out. I heard that one large company was hiring for warehouse workers. I knew I could do that, and I was somewhat heartened by the fact that it wasn't going to require a lot of decision-making on my part, that I could sort of do it on autopilot, and that would free me to give lots of thought to planning my next step.

I went to the distribution center, filled out an application, turned it in, and waited to be interviewed on the spot. I was called in by a really disinterested HR lady, who scanned my information, asked me no questions whatsoever about why I wanted the job or anything else, but just told me to return to that same office next Wednesday between 8:00am and noon.

The next Wednesday I was there bright and early, certain that I would finally get the in-depth interview I had been expecting. Once again, an HR rep called me in, asked me if I was interested in the job, I said "Yes," and she said for me to come back the next Wednesday. She made a little note on my file that I had come in as instructed.

You get where this is going, don't you? I went to that office every Wednesday for a month, just going in, sitting in the lobby, waiting for the HR person to give me my checkmark. After about the fifth week of this, I received a call that I had been accepted and to come in for orientation.

> ...
> **Find out before the end of the interview how you are expected to maintain contact.**
> ...

This was the ritual that was in place for that particular company to determine if a candidate was actually interested in that job. If I had failed to show up one Wednesday, I would have been removed from the eligibility list. If I had chosen to call them, week in and week out, they would have felt harassed and my chances would have disappeared. If I had come in and hung out in the office on days other than Wednesday, they probably would have had Security escort me out. This Wednesday ritual was part of the corporate culture and could not be changed.

The point of all of this is: Find out before the end of the interview how you are expected to maintain contact. Ask, "May I call you in a week (or whatever) to follow up?" If they are willing for you to do that, and if they say so, then it's okay to call the company. If they act pained at the idea of you calling to check on your application, that means *leave them alone*! They'll call you if they're interested. There can be nothing that spells out desperation more than constant phone messages. Bureaucracy is a big, slow beast. It moves with the speed of a hippopotamus. Know that, accept it, wait it out. You want them to think that you have so much going on right now that it's cool if they can't get back to you for a month. *I* know you're desperate. *You* know you're desperate. Don't let *them* know it.

> ...
> **There can be nothing that spells out desperation more than constant phone messages. Bureaucracy is a big, slow beast.**
> ...

14

You're an Old Geezer, Aren't You?

Issues of Age, Sex, Ethnicity, Disability and Other Reasons for Discrimination

When I walked into the interview, I saw 10 people seated at a long meeting room table. I was pretty sure that not a single person in that room topped out at over the age of 30, maybe 32. I knew from that first moment that this was the killing fields for me.

I had gone to interview for a job with the federal government's Social Security Administration. Somehow it had never occurred to me that an agency that deals exclusively with the aged and infirm would be staffed so totally by young people. This was a gang-bang I would not soon forget.

The leading youngster there began the interview with the standard question about myself, following it up, of course, with the strengths and weaknesses questions, and then one young dude decided to pull out all stops and ask the following question, and I quote here, word for word: "Think _way, way_ back to your first job and tell me something you learned from it."

I'm not sure how you would have interpreted that, but it was, to me, a very apparent attack on my age. In spite of the fact that they had my very impressive resume in front of them, the whole demeanor of this panel, followed by this blatant ageist question, was like fingernails on a chalkboard to me. This was a showdown. It was clear that I wasn't going to get the job. So, I figured, I might as well have a little fun with it.

My answer was something along the lines of "Well, first of all, I have to tell you that if you really wanted to ask my age, you should have come right out and asked it. But since you didn't, I'll just answer your question. I learned from my first job that just as soon as we could get electricity it would change the way all of us did our jobs and we could throw away our candlesticks." I was not hired.

Ageism

Ageism is everywhere, along with sexism, racism, and more isms than we can even list. Every moment we live gives rise to a new form of discrimination. Our world is rife with it. I grew up hearing about how wonderful the Asian countries were because they took care of their elderly people and re-vered their knowledge and experience. Old people were close to being holy. I kind of liked that and even looked forward to some extent to when that attitude would reach America and I would be treated with respect. Young people would gather around me in groups and listen raptly as I spoke from my wealth of wisdom. It was going to be great! I'm still waiting to see that happen.

Sexism

Sexism shouldn't be a problem anymore, but it still is, al-though to a lesser extent than 20 years ago. Back in the six-ties, women were thought to be incapable of driving a police car and performing the duties of an active field officer. We were expected to work as babysitters in the Youth Unit or, after Crimes Against Persons expanded to include things like

Special Victims units, women were moved to deal with what were considered strictly crimes against women.

Prior to that time, officers referred to an incident of rape as a "non-pay." If a woman was raped, it was assumed that she had brought it upon herself. Men didn't want to deal with such incidents and, at least from my experience with them, most of our male officers had little compassion for the victims. Women were given the jobs the men didn't want to do.

Women's groups have made real strides since those days and women can work practically everywhere now, except in the starting lineup of the NFL. Many women now serve at the highest levels of government, with some actively seeking the presidency.

We still, however, are limited by what experts call the Glass Ceiling, which means that we can advance only so far in the corporate world before our gender stops us in our tracks before reaching the highest pay grades and levels of accomplishment. Estrogen is still our enemy.

Gays and lesbians have been on a roller coaster of victimization, tolerance, victimization, acceptance, victimization…I think we're back to tolerance? I'm not really sure, as of this moment. This group has experienced a volatile history in our country when it comes to making any kind of progress toward equality and probably will continue in this vein for decades to come.

Racism

Racism has made great strides since the days of Martin Luther King, and the mere fact that we now have a bi-racial president is evidence that a majority of opinion has changed for the better in this country. Laws have been enacted at all levels of government to deal with issues of racism. Although I'm sure there are still pockets of hatred, based on geographic areas, racial purity theories, and an inability to forget the Civil War, most of this country exhibits attitudes of racial tolerance. Intermarriage is commonplace. Acceptance is increasingly a national attitude.

Language and Communication Intolerance(ism)

If you speak with a foreign accent or your English is difficult to understand, expect to be discriminated against in the job market. Many jobs require excellent communication skills, and the language of communication in the American workplace is English. Whether you like it or not, it's your responsibility to improve your language skills, and that includes everything from speaking in clear English to using proper grammar and complete sentences. It's not "cool" in most workplaces to speak with a heavy foreign accent or use low-class street language. If you lack good English language skills, you will appear uneducated and less than competent in today's demanding workplace.

> ...
> **Acceptance is increasingly a national attitude.**
> ...

Disability Dislike(ism)

Strangely enough, disability is harder to actually determine than ever before in our history. Our laws have changed to define what constitutes legal disability, but it's beginning to appear that every single one of us is in some way disabled. Today disabilities go beyond just the obvious physical disabilities associated with mobility, hearing, and sight. They also include a host of learning and mental disabilities, such as ADD (Attention Deficit Disorder), ADHD (Attention Deficit and Hyperactive Disorder), PTSD (Post Traumatic Stress Disorder), bipolarity, depression, and a variety of addictive behaviors.

Our children have ADD by the thousands. That means that they can't pay attention in school and that's the reason they're having trouble learning. ADD is a legal disability. If the kids don't have ADD, they're autistic, a disability that I can't even pretend to understand. All I know is the number of autistic children who will grow up to be autistic adults is growing larger all the time. Disabled.

> ...
> **Many jobs require excellent communication skills. It's your responsibility to improve your language skills.**
> ...

Carpal tunnel syndrome is a disability, and most of us who have held office jobs already have it. If you type on a keyboard all day, play too many video games each day, do any kind of intricate work with your fingers, or perform any repetitive motion day in and day out, you will probably end up with nerve damage in your wrist and arm. Carpal tunnel syndrome. Disabled.

And these disabilities aren't even the ones we've always known about, the ones with foundations, telethons, wheelchairs, summer camps, and firemen collecting change in their big fireperson boots at the intersections. But they are all disabilities.

So what does that mean? From an employment standpoint, it means that there are thousands upon thousands of people who technically cannot be denied employment, but who, in reality, will be turned away from jobs because of those disabilities. Oh, the companies won't admit that's the reason. They'll use some other excuse, like, "Not a team player," "Not a good job match."

-Isms

I wish I had better news here, because I have been discriminated against in employment several times over like so many of the rest of you. I'm physically disabled, as well as being chronologically disabled. I know I still have much to contribute to society. I still want to work, to help people like you, but my avenues of doing that are growing fewer and fewer each day. The faster I move toward that Ultimate Incinerator, the more I feel for people who are just in their forties and are already being treated "old." The lines you read in fashion magazines, like "Fifty is the New Forty," serve only to get you to buy the magazines. The truth is, if you're over 40, you're probably over, at least from an employment standpoint. I'm sorry.

> ...
> **The truth is, if you're over 40, you're probably over, at least from an employment standpoint. I'm sorry.**
> ...

Many older Americans believe they are not getting jobs because the young kids are running the corporations. Gays and lesbians are being persecuted just for being. Women are not being able to advance to their full potential in business. Disabled people are not being hired for jobs they should be able to do by companies fearing their "special" circumstances. English-challenged foreign-born job-seekers are unable to land or perform jobs because they lack important communication skills.

I'm not in favor of any kind of discrimination. Really, I'm not. But the more we all become "special," in one way or the other, the less anybody is.

15

So You Got the Job, Big Whoop!

Now That You've Got the Job, You've Got to DO the Job—Mistakes Employees Make to End Up Unemployed Again

"Employers hire for skills…and fire for behaviors."

You got the job! Great! It's been a long time coming, hasn't it? Now that you've got it, are you going to keep it? It depends to a large degree on how you handle these four most critical indicators of job longevity:

- time management
- attitude
- performance
- property

Now that you work for Company XYZ, you're going to be expected to become an XYZer, embracing the corporate culture and obeying all of the rules and regulations that are inherent in that. Most companies consider coming on board a great honor and they will be watching you like a hawk to make sure you are truly going to fit in. That's why so many of them have that "probationary period" during which every breath you take, every move you make, every bond you break, they'll be watching you.

Time Management

You just started a new job, and you now have a work schedule that perhaps isn't exactly what you hoped it would be. If you've always worked days and now you're on the night shift, it might present problems that you've never had to deal with before. Maybe it's a matter of child care, perhaps sleep habits, but whatever it is, it's going to take adjustment.

I experienced this when I went from a desk job to working a very strange shift as a Security Screener at the airport. I had to get up at 1:30am to get ready for work because I had an hour's drive to the airport, then I had to catch a shuttle bus from the employees' parking lot to the terminal, then I had to be in the crew room to time-in and for security updates at 4:00am and have the gate completely checked out for security and ready to open at 5:00am. I loved that job, but it was hard on my "real" life. I got off of work at 12:30pm, was home by about 1:30pm or 2:00pm, did a few things around the house, prepared dinner for my husband, and by 5:30pm or 6:00pm I was in bed.

> ...
> **Working and surviving a less-than-ideal schedule is, in many companies, considered a rite of passage.**
> ...

Any change of schedule takes its toll on our bodies and our minds. It takes complete readjustment both physically and mentally. When I first started that job, I actually quit during the training because I just didn't think I was going to be able to make it work. I gave it some thought for a couple of days, went crawling back and begged them to let me try it again. It finally clicked, and I look back on that job as being the most fun I've ever had on a job.

The company is trusting you to accept the fact that your beginning schedule may not be ideal for you. Working and surviving a less-than-ideal schedule is, in many companies, considered a rite of passage. Paying your dues. Sometimes it's weird hours like I had. Sometimes it's the absolute, non-negotiable fact that you will have to work some or even all weekends. Sometimes it's holidays that most of us really want to spend with our families but now we don't get off anymore.

Okay, the schedule isn't good, but let's look at it this way. You can work the schedule, put in your time, and get to a place where you can bid on a better schedule, or you can quit and spend all of your time at home, like you've been doing for so long. Your choice.

The company is going to be looking at how you manage time. They will watch your punctuality and see if you report to work on time, if you leave early, if you take long breaks and lunches. These things are almost always issues in companies where you're working side by side with other workers who will be happy to report you if you take longer breaks than they do.

Your bosses will be required to keep track of your attendance and, if you take off more than the company's regulations allow, they will "write you up" for poor attendance. Being "written up" is almost always the precursor to being fired. Sometimes it takes several such incidents, sometimes not, but beware the first write-up because that usually begins a campaign of scrutiny that is hard to shake.

Attitude

When you start working for a company, you will usually be given a copy of that company's employee handbook. This outlines the company's rules and regulations and governs the conduct of all employees. Consider it the company's Ten Commandments. If you disobey any of these, those actions could be considered grounds for termination.

Among those commandments will be topics like sexual harassment, the conditions under which you can be written up, and basic standards for job performance. Somewhere in here will be clauses that have to do with you getting along with your co-workers, obeying the direct orders of your supervisor, and just plain not stepping on anybody's toes.

You will be expected to keep a positive attitude, to not bitch and moan when given an order by your supervisor that doesn't necessarily make sense to you. You are being paid to perform functions, not to figure out why you are supposed to do them. "Ours is not to wonder why, ours is but to do and die…"

> **...**
> **Be friendly, be helpful, but be as private as you can possibly be.**
> **...**

You will be expected to work alongside your co-workers, which means getting along well with everybody. Try it, it's not as easy as it sounds! The key to making this work most of the time is to keep your personal life as much to yourself as possible. I speak from experience. There is an old saying that goes, "Familiarity breeds contempt." It also breeds gossip and personal judgments. Be friendly, be helpful, but be as private as you can possibly be.

Performance

The main reason you're there is to work. You're going to be paid to perform at a certain level and up to a certain standard of quality. In manufacturing or warehouse settings, this usually equates to production quotas: so many frickfracks produced in so many minutes. Production quality standards mean that those frickfracks must measure up to at least minimum standards of frickfrack durability and quality. You, as part of this production cycle, will be expected to hold up your end of the deal, working at the pace that is set for the assembly line. These standards have been studied and set by Certified Engineers in Technical Fields, and they know a whole lot better than you every knowable fact about frickfrack production, so suck it up and do your portion. You don't want to hold up the line!

> ...
> **Probationary periods—six months, nine months, maybe even a year—are standard at most companies.**
> ...

The same concept is true regardless of what kind of job you take. If you work in an office, your part of the workload will be pre-determined. If you're a bartender, you'll be expected to handle the bar either by yourself or with the assistance of another person, depending on the size of the establishment. But you get the idea. Whatever your job is, somebody higher up has figured out how much work they expect you to perform and how long it should take you to do it. You will be measured on your ability to meet those expectations.

Property

Your company is your new home and you will be expected to treat it with the respect you want others to show in your own place. You will be expected to take care of their equipment, offices, or workspaces, and you will most definitely be expected to honor the fact that the supplies and equipment you use at work don't actually belong to you, personally. The office supplies were purchased to use in the office.

The tools in the workshop need to stay in the workshop, and anything you use to do the job needs to be maintained in a usable condition. If you drive a company truck, you need to be responsible for making sure it gets to the proper people for routine maintenance on a regular basis. If you work with computers, you will be expected to use those computers only for the purpose for which they were provided. The company's property belongs to the company

> ...
> **Human Resources representatives are not your friends.**
> ...

and it's sacred. Thou shalt not covet, thou shalt not steal, and thou shalt not troll for porn on company computers during thine lunch break!

Probationary Periods

If you commit some sort of infraction, you may feel that you're being picked on. If you haven't completed your probationary period, the chances are good that you're right. Probationary periods—six months, nine months, maybe even a year—are standard at most companies. Think of them as college "hazing" or initiation ceremonies. They are events and periods of time during which your resolve to learn the job and fit in at the company are being tested. Some supervisors throw the crappiest busy-work jobs they can find at a new hire, just because they can and to see how the new person reacts. If you really want the job, you'll roll with it. If you don't, you'll take it to Human Resources.

Okay, here I go again, being unkind to Human Resources professionals everywhere, but, speaking from experience, I can say that Human Resources representatives are not your friends. Get that? *Not your friends.* Do not assume that you can go to the office of an HR rep and spill your guts and receive sympathy about the ugly things being done to you in your job. They are **not your friends** and **they don't care**. They are paid by the **company** to represent the **company**. That means they will not do or say anything that could come back to bite them if you end up getting terminated and want to sue them for Wrongful Termination, Discrimination, or any other legally actionable charge. HR representatives are there to pass on pertinent benefit information or behavior regulations from the company's handbooks or other published sources. That's all they can do for you. Don't expect them to intercede with your supervisor on your behalf. It's just not going to happen. If you take a problem to HR, you're going to end up with yet another memo in your personnel folder (and you may not even know about it) that can't do you any good. Don't trust Human Resources. They're not there for you.

The Beginning of the End

It happens all the time. People land jobs, get comfortable, start relaxing and being themselves. They don't show up for work or they're late all the time. They fail to call in or call in with no good reason. They abuse break schedules. They get into altercations—verbal or otherwise—with co-workers. They sass their supervisors. They fall down on production or quality standards. They steal from the company. They abuse company property. The list actually goes on and on.

It makes no sense. You went through hell and high water to find a job. Why would you jeopardize your future and the well-being of your family to commit any of these indiscretions? Here's today's workplace reality: **Every breath you take, every move you make, every bond you break, they'll be watching you.**

16
I Was F@!#ing Fired!

The Ungrateful Pigs Divorced
You From Their Company

I was just sittin' there, eatin' my lunch, when Zippy comes over and tells me Earl wants to see me in the office. So, I go in the office and he just turns around and says 'Roy, you been comin' in late and you're not keepin' up with the rest of the guys, so you're outta here.' Just like that. No warnin', no nothin'."

Wow, how many times do I hear that a day? Well, not exactly the saga of Roy and Earl, but similar stories. One of the main issues here is the question of whether or not Roy was fired or laid off. It's important to know because it will mean the difference between Roy being able to draw unemployment benefits or having to get a cardboard box to write a begging sign on.

> ...
> **Thousands of employees who are "let go" aren't aware of whether they were "downsized" or "divorced."**
> ...

Many times, employers don't make it clear to the newly "divorced" ex-employee that they are actually being fired. Maybe the supervisor really hates to have to take the action and wants to soften the blow a bit, or maybe the employer is just hoping the issue won't come up and they won't end up somehow in a Wrongful Termination lawsuit. For whatever reason, literally thousands of employees who are "let go" aren't aware of whether they were "downsized" or "divorced."

What's the difference? Downsizing is a normally legitimate personnel action made necessary due to downturns in business, seasonal factors that make work impossible to complete, or just plain carrying too many employees for the earning potential of the company. There are numerous reasons why companies choose to downsize, and the employees affected are considered "laid off." Under such circumstances, these individuals are normally entitled to file for and receive unemployment benefits through the state in which they were employed. Normally.

The whole scenario changes if the employee is not downsized but is in fact "divorced." There are a whole group of words that are used to describe this action, but the most common among them are "fired," "terminated," and "separated." I prefer to call such an action a "corporate divorce" because that's exactly what it feels like. They don't love you anymore. They don't want to see your face or have you present in their corporate life. Take your toys and leave. Quietly, please.

The pain is not unlike a divorce. You may not have seen it coming. You may not have been "written up," which could at least prepare you for the possibility that your relationship may soon be over. If you had anticipated this, you could have taken whatever action the boss thought was necessary to correct the problem and restore you to the company's good graces. If that wasn't a good option, you could have started looking for another job and maybe found one, turned in a decent notice, and left without the stigma of being fired on your record. But, nooooo, they decided it would be better to just drop the bomb on you and get you off the property.

To add insult to injury, they may also decide that, because of whatever heinous act you committed, you are not worthy to receive unemployment benefits, which would at least provide a financial stipend for you to live on until you find another job. Maybe it's because they actually believe that you are guilty of some infraction of the rules and that you deliberately committed it. It's possible that they feel righteously justified about making your life a living hell after kicking you out. Or maybe they just want to deprive you of unemployment benefits **because they can**.

It is the right of the employer in most, if not all, states to protest the issuance of unemployment benefits to a separated employee. After an individual files for benefits, the state contacts the employer to determine the circumstances under which the employee was let go. If the employer is convincing in making a case that supports termination, those benefits can be denied because unemployment benefits are paid to workers who are terminated **through no fault of their own**.

The state would then contact the employee to hear their side of the story. At some point in time, a hearing is usually conducted—either a telephone conference call or in person—with the individual, a representative of the company, and an official arbitrator for the state. After hearing both sides of the story, the arbitrator makes a decision as to whether the benefits would be paid.

Some companies make a habit of protesting the payment of benefits. It's just their corporate culture and tradition. They rationalize that if benefits are refused, it will save the company money somehow, since they actually have to pay into unemployment for each employee on the company payroll. For whatever reason, some companies just don't believe that some people deserve to receive it. They may also believe that the person involved won't take the case any further if they're turned down. If the separated employee so desires and has the money or connections to hook up with a willing attorney, they can file a Wrongful Termination lawsuit and possibly end up with a nice little settlement plus the contested unemployment payments.

It's vital to know exactly which category you're in if you're "let go." Make the company put it in writing. Tell them that you need a document before you leave that states whether you are being laid off or fired. You have a right to know and you're going to **need** to know. It's going to make a big difference in what benefits and services will be available to you after you clear out your locker and turn in your company ID.

> ...
> **You need a document before you leave that states whether you are being laid off or fired. It's going to make a big difference in benefits and services.**
> ...

If your health or life insurance is carried by the company, you're going to need to know if you have the right to continue that insurance as a COBRA account, where you will continue paying a larger portion of the premiums and the company will pay their portion for a designated amount of time following your termination. This benefit isn't usually available to individuals who are fired, only laid off.

If you have a significant amount of time with the company, the option of being retired rather than laid off may have existed, but if you're fired rather than retired, you may stand to lose many privileges of those who have served honorably. When the large card company I worked for decided that they needed to start downsizing and they cut my job, I was "re-tired" because I had 20 years of service with the company. What that means is I still have some company benefits, in-cluding a significant discount on their products, and I can still come back and walk through the building, visiting some of my old cronies if I so desire. If I had been fired instead of retired, I would have lost those benefits.

The circumstances of your corporate "divorce" are vitally important. Make sure you know what they are. Make sure you are careful of what documents you sign before you leave, because signing a paper agreeing to whatever language the company has provided could ultimately cheat you out of un-employment benefits or the rights of redress should you de-cide to sue. Be especially careful if the bomb is dropped on you without warning. You will be in a state of shock and will usually sign anything they put in front of you because they'll convince you that you are better off signing the form and go-ing away quietly. You're not. Don't sign anything without the advice of an attorney, even if it means telling them that you'll be back with your attorney to discuss the circumstances under which you'll be willing to sign their forms. Protect yourself!

> ...
> **Don't sign anything without the advice of an attorney.**
> ...

All right, the worst has hap-pened and you're out of a job. You're looking for work, you're getting a few leads. You've written a good resume and now you've actually lined up an inter-view. How do you discuss the fact that your last company booted you out?

It's all in the words you choose to use. As I said earlier, "fired" can also be "terminated" or "separated." Since most of us already equate "fired" with "terminated," the use of the word "separated" has a less negative connotation, simply by virtue of lack of use. When you fill out that job application, and it asks for the reason you left the job, you can use "Separated." Until the HR representative actually has you in front of them, exactly what "separated" means is up in the air. They're going to need to ask you what you meant by "separated" and that will occur in an interview.

As I've said before, the interview is where you have to sell yourself and your skills. When you're asked what you mean by "separated," you're going to use language that does not in any way indicate anger toward your former employer. I'm not saying that you should lie. I'm just saying there are ways of blandly indicating that you had differences of opinion that led to your departure. You can say something like "It wasn't a good job fit," "We had differences of interpretation in the instructions I was given," or "Changes in management or job structure resulted in a difficult work environment."

Clearly, this won't work if you were accused of stealing or some other obvious criminal activity, but if you ended up in a situation where you were working for a boss who didn't like you or if you experienced some other personality clash with co-workers, these are the most diplomatic ways to get around providing details. If you were accused of criminal activity, you're going to have to tell the interviewer about it, but you'll probably plead innocence. There's no easy way to discuss this reason for termination. You'll have to throw yourself on the mercy of the court.

Downsizing is a common corporate tool in this economy. As I stated in an earlier chapter, companies are looking at employees who are nearing retirement with full benefits, and they're targeting them for termination before that golden date arrives. It's tacky, it's mean, it's downright evil. But it's usually legal. If they can find a reason that isn't out-and-out actionable, they'll use it to avoid paying out benefits over time to someone no longer clocking in each day. The days of corporate loyalty to employees are pretty much gone.

...

The days of corporate loyalty to employees are pretty much gone.

...

I tell my clients to try not to take it personally. I know it isn't easy, and I've definitely been in their shoes. They should, however, recognize the realities of the economy we're in right now and acknowledge that they are part of a great restructuring that is going on in many aspects of American industry, economy, and job market.

17

Light at the End of the Tunnel

Yes, There is Some...Not Much, But Some

*"You must consent to lose sight
of land for a very long time in order
to discover new worlds."*

W hen the participants of the Ex-Offenders Workshop enter the room where I teach it, the lights are off and a large slide is projected on the white wall. The image is a seascape, with a view from the rocky cliff over-looking the ocean, gazing out to sea. The caption reads, "You must consent to lose sight of land for a very long time in order to discover new worlds." I tell my clients that it has nothing and everything to do with what they came to learn.

My students come to learn about change, the changes they need to make in order to become productive, employed members of society again. It's going to take a lot of work and it's natural that they're going to experience a lot of fear. So I tell them about this quote, paraphrased from Andre Gide.

There is a story behind that quote. When I left law enforcement, I was plain terrified. I couldn't do it anymore, but I couldn't live without it either. Somewhere around that time, I saw that quote, although I don't remember the exact words, hence the paraphrasing. I'm a history lover, and when I read the exact words by Gide, they made me think of the explorers in their wooden sailing ships, those old galleons they sailed away in from Europe to discover new continents. At the time, they were told the world was flat, that they would eventually sail right off the edge. Map-makers, not knowing what lay beyond a certain point on the map, simply printed the legend "Here there be dragons."

Still, these explorers, in their rickety little wooden sailing vessels, set off for parts unknown, trading the security of land and everything they had ever taken for granted for what they had been told would be imminent destruction. They believed totally in themselves, their ships, and their missions. They sailed away on belief alone. As history records, some succeeded, some didn't.

> ...
> **We have to give up the security of everything we've ever known in order to reinvent ourselves.**
> ...

This same scenario is true for all of us today. We have to give up the security of everything we've ever known in order to reinvent ourselves. The ex-offenders I teach have to give up all association with people and places from their past. They have to learn completely new lines of work. Maybe that's true for you, too. Maybe, because your particular line of work is in decline or completely gone, you'll have to learn a totally new trade in an "in-demand" field. Maybe you'll have to uproot yourself and your family to move to a city that has employment opportunities for you. Maybe you have to go back to school just to beef up on the latest information in the field that you're already in.

Whatever the situation, it's going to involve some degree of modification of your life, and that means giving up sight of the "land" you have always thought of as home. You're going to have to get in your little wooden ship and sail off into the unknown in order to discover the new world that will be your new life. It's scary. Downright terrifying, in fact. None of us have a clue just how much worse the economy or the world in general will get. We're making this up as we go along.

What is indisputably true is that there's no going back to the good old days we knew. We have to prepare to move forward or fall by the wayside. I know. You're saying, "But how am I supposed to survive while I'm making these changes?" This isn't going to be pretty, but here it comes.

> **...**
> **Social programs are in place for people in need.**
> **...**

You are going to admit that this is no time for pride. If your family needs food stamps to get by, you file for the food stamps. If you have children with special needs, you contact organizations that support those disabilities to see if they can help. You apply for any and all assistance available wherever you live. If you're on unemployment, you comply, without fail, with the guidelines in place for that program. If you receive food stamps and are required to do documented job searches in order to receive those food stamps, you do it, and you do it faithfully and without embarrassment. Social programs are in place for people in need, and if you're out of work and your family is hungry, honey, you're a person in need. You do whatever it takes, legally, to provide for your family. And don't ever, ever, ever consider committing a felony for that same purpose. No one ever wins in a situation like that. **No one!**

There is a Chinese curse that says, "May you live in interesting times." Well, these are exceptionally interesting times.

None of us would wish them upon anyone. However, we are here at this time and in this place. We can't change that.

I'm just a workforce professional who sees these scenarios day in and day out, and I'd certainly like to be put out of business. It would be wonderful if everybody had the jobs they need and there was no one left that I would have to counsel in this way. As long as there is, I'm going to keep trying to teach people to become more employable job candidates, and I will continue to preach change at people while at the same time urging them to try to keep their spirits up.

I grew up really poor. My mother had three children and was divorced from a man who was absent from our lives in presence and support. At one point in time, we had no furniture, no dishes, nothing. We would buy a carton of milk, pass it around until all the milk was gone, and then we would cut off the top, creating a bowl. Enough cut-off milk cartons and we had almost an entire serving set of dishes. We were dirt poor, but you know what? My memories of those early years were some of my most treasured, the happiest times of my life. We were close then, and it taught me the importance of what we are to each other and the need to rely on those we love. We became survivors, and all us need to become survivors today.

> ...
> **A little bit of hardship builds character.**
> ...

A little bit of hardship builds character. There's too much emphasis on material things in our world today and not enough on who we are deep inside or who we should be as citizens of this country. We need to get back to a time when we treasure each other and our freedoms more than our toys. We need to cherish the idea that when times get rough, we have the right to make our own choices. America is blessed in that way more than any other nation on earth. Each man or woman is the CEO of his or her own destiny. If we can accept that, take responsibility for it and live accordingly, then we can be said to be people of good character.

> ...
> **Each man or woman is the CEO of his or her own destiny.**
> ...

We have to bravely move forward with our individual goals, letting go of our old security blankets, consenting to leave behind the sight of land and all we used to take for granted, in order to discover our new worlds. The journey will be challenging. Indeed, like a good sailor and the captain of the ship, you have a destination in mind, but the exact route of your journey will be affected by how well you handle your environment. You may be buffeted by winds that occasionally blow you off course, but as you improve your navigation skills, you will become master of your ship.

This sailing analogy is appropriate for anyone facing unemployment and looking for a job. While we currently face a miserable job market in a sucky economy, that doesn't mean you have to become a victim of this situation. If you change your attitude and approach to job hunting, which I've noted throughout this book, you will move on to better days. This book hopefully will get you started on a new chapter in your life.

APPENDICES

Appendix A: Selected Job Search Information Websites

Careers: http://www.careers.org

Kansas Works: https://kansasworks.com/ada

Kansas Civil Service Jobs: http://www.da.ks.gov/ps/aaa/recruitment

Kansas Career Pipeline: http://www.kansascareerpipeline.org/

JobFit: https://kansas.jobfit.com/jfwibmain.aspx?id=HWORKS

Missouri Career Source: https://www.missouricareersource.com/mcs/mcs/default.seek

Oklahoma Job Link: https://servicelink.oesc.state.ok.us/ada

Nebraska Works: http://NEworks.nebraska.gov

Colorado Workforce: http://coloradojobs.cdle.org

The Ladders (jobs paying over $100,000): http://www.theladders.com

Jobs in Sports: http://www.jobsinsports.com

CareerBuilder (used by KC Star and Lawrence Journal-World): http://www.careerbuilder.com

Job Bank USA: http://www.jobbankusa.com

USA Jobs (Federal job site): http://www.usajobs.opm.gov

Kelly Services: http://www.kellyservices.com

Net Temps: http://net-temps.com

Manpower: http://www.manpower.com

AppleOne: http://www.appleone.com

Westaff: http://www.westaff.com

MyHuey: http://www.myhuey.com

Kansas City Jobs: http://www.kcjobs.com

Nation Job: http://www.nationjob.com

Jobs Opportunity: http://jobsopportunity.net

The Chronicle of Higher Education: http://chronicle.com

Animal Science Jobs: http://www.animalsciencejobs.com

Science Careers: http://sciencecareers.sciencemag.org

Nonprofit Jobs: http://npconnect.org

Jobs Online: http://www.jobsonline.com

Go Jobs: http://www.gojobs.com

SnagAJob: http://www.snagajob.com

Simply Hired: http://www.simplyhired.com

Job.com: http://www.job.com

Monster.com: http://www.monster.com

Indeed.com: http://www.indeed.com

Missouri Economic Research and Information Center (MERIC): http://www.missourieconomy.org

My Skills, My Future (free assessments): http://www.myskillsmyfuture.org

TheBeehive (for ex-offenders): http://thebeehive.org

JailtoJobs (for ex-offenders): http://jailtojobs.com

Hard2Hire (for ex-offenders): http://hard2hire.com

ExOffender Reentry (for ex-offenders): http://exoffender
reentry.com

Free tutorials for the inexperienced computer user:

iTyping: www.nimblefingers.com

Mouse: www.pbclibrary.org/mousing

Free online tutorials for using Microsoft Word, Excel, Power
Point, etc.: http://www.baycongroup.com/tutorials.htm

Website for free typing practice and typing and 10-key
speeds: http://www.learn2type.com

Appendix B: Free Email Account

The following example explains how to set up a free Yahoo email account. Other popular free email accounts can be set up through Gmail (mail.gmail.com) and Hotmail (www.hot mail.com).

Setting Up An Email Account

Go to www.yahoo.com

Screen 1:

1. Click on "New here? Sign up"

2. Complete Section 1.
   Enter personal information: First name, last name, gender, birthday, country, postal code.

3. Complete Section 2.
   Select an ID and Password…The system will display suggestions.

4. Complete Section 3.
   " In case you forget your ID or password…" Leave the "Alternate Email" section blank. Select a Secret Question from the dropdown menu; type in your answer on the line below. Select a second Secret Question from the dropdown menu; type in your answer on the line below.

5. "Type in the code shown" (Will be a strangely skewed sequence of letters and/or numbers.) If you can't read the code, you can click on the box that says "Try a new code" and a new one will appear, letting you try again.

6. Click on "Create My Account."

Screen 2:

1. The system will bring up a confirmation screen, show-ing the details of your account. Print this, if possible. Also, write your password on the sheet, because this is not printed out in the confirmation.

2. Click on "Continue" to sign in to Yahoo!

Screen 3:

1. Click on "Mail" tab to view emails, then click on "In-box."

2. Click on email title to read the message.

3. Click on "Compose" tab to compose a new email message.

4. Click on "Send" tab to send the email.

Accessing an Email Account

Go to www.yahoo.com

1. Click on "Sign in."

2. Enter Yahoo! ID and Password. (Be sure to put "@yahoo.com" at the end of your ID.)

3. Click on "Enter."

4. Click on "Mail" tab to view emails, then click on "In-box."

5. Click on email title to read the message.

6. Click on "Compose" tab to compose a new email message.

7. Click on "Send" tab to send the email.

User ID: _____

Password: _____

Appendix C: Sample Resumes

Functional Resume

BEVERLY COLE STAFFORD
2723 Winchester Road
Oakley, MO 55555
(999) 999-9999
BevColeStaf@yahoo.com

PROFESSIONAL SUMMARY

Certified Nurse Aide and Dietary Specialist with nine years' experience working in diet and nutrition in institutional settings. Highly developed interpersonal and customer service skills.

SKILLS

- ✓ Advised patients, their families, and groups on nutritional principles, dietary plans and diet modifications, food selection and preparation and nutritional quality of life improvements
- ✓ Tested new food products and equipment
- ✓ Developed policies for food service and nutritional programs to assist in health promotion and disease control
- ✓ Coordinated recipe development and standardization and developed new menus for independent food service operations
- ✓ Consulted with physicians and health care personnel to determine nutritional needs and diet restrictions of patient and client
- ✓ Purchased food in accordance with health and safety codes and ensured compliance with health department standards for kitchen operation

EXPERIENCE

Premier Assistance, Oakley, MO	*Dietary Aide*	5/2007 to 10/2009
Armour Ridge Medical Center, Claymore, MO	*Dietary Aide*	6/2003 to 5/2007
Cannady Place Retirement Home, Lexington,MO	*Dietary Aide*	1/1997 to 6/2003

EDUCATION

Westminster College, Cafton, MO	*Certified Nurse Aide,*
Wright Career College, Coffeyville, KS	*Accounting II Certification*
Women's Employment Network, Gilmore, MO	*Horizons Program Certification*

Reverse-Chronological Resume

BRYAN LATHROP
2495 Crockett Lane
Sioux City, IA
(999) 999-9999
BryanLath@gmail.com

SKILLS SUMMARY

Experience includes sales, customer service, administrative/clerical support and management. Communicates well with all types of people. Versatile, flexible, reliable. PC proficient in Windows, Word, Excel and PowerPoint.

EMPLOYMENT HISTORY

Calais Club, Sioux City, IA   July 2009 to Present
Bartender/Doorman
Provide superior customer service by serving drinks to customers as well as by providing security for the club.

University of Iowa, Cedar Rapids, IA   January, 2007 to January, 2009
Receptionist (Work-Study Position)
Answered multi-line telephone in the Chancellor's office. Filed paperwork. Assisted students with completing financial aid applications.

Boromir Chevrolet, Cedar Falls , IA   November, 2006 to October, 2007
Salesperson
Demonstrated features of and sold vehicles. Prospected for new customers. Trained others.
Achievements: Sold on average 15 vehicles a month.

Casey Flynn Shoes, Cedar Falls, IA   March, 2005 to September, 2006
Assistant Manager
Sold shoes and provided customer service. Organized merchandise displays. Managed stock. Assisted with hiring. Trained others.
Achievements: Consistently ranked as highest salesperson.

Ethridge Marketing Associates, Cedar Falls, IA   July, 2004 to February, 2005
Telemarketer
Placed outbound calls to prospective clients on behalf of contract businesses.

EDUCATION

Southwest High School, Des Moines, IA
High School Diploma

Functional Resume

DAMIAN STARKEY
4690 El Cerito Lindo
Los Angeles, CA 55555
Cell: (999) 999-9999
Home: ((999) 999-9999
Email: Dstarkeyjr@hotmail.com

KNOWLEDGE AND SKILLS

Supervisory Skills:
- Customer service and complaint management skills
- Trouble-shooting and customer satisfaction follow-up
- Supervisory skills, including staff scheduling and performance evaluation
- Sales skills in retail and service provision
- Retail store operations skills, including inventory control
- Fast food management
- Computer skills (Windows, Word, Excel, PowerPoint, Auto Cad, Micro Station, Internet knowledgeable)

Technical/Professional Skills:
- Inspect construction sites
- Conduct concrete tests for structural integrity of concrete
- Conduct concrete cylinder tests for quality of concrete
- Conduct soil tests to determine compaction and stability
- Conduct core drilling in the ground
- Responsible for OSHA reporting
- Supervision of construction crews
- Knowledge of safety requirements for construction sites
- Knowledge of building requirements for construction of bridges/roads
- Knowledge of working and safety for construction equipment
- Knowledge of requirements/laws governed by Department of Transportation
- Knowledge of federal, state and local zoning governing construction of roads and bridges

WORK EXPERIENCE

Blakely Personnel	Technical Inspector	El Cerito Lindo, CA
Lawn Masters Lawn Care	Service Route Manager	Tempe, AZ
Discount Mart	Assistant Manager	Westchester, AZ
Nicholson Staffing	Field Representative	Plainsboro, MO
Missouri Department of Transportation	Senior Construction Technician	Seven Oaks, MO

EDUCATION

Lincoln University, Brownsville, MO
Bachelors of Science Degree in Civil Engineering Technology

Lincoln University, Brownsville, MO
Associates Degree in Architectural Drafting and Architectural CAD/CADD

Combination Resume

GORDON CASSIDY
2023 Harrison Avenue
Ocean View, NJ 55555
(999) 999-9999

WORK EXPERIENCE

Rathburn Rubber, Pasaic, NJ   5/2009 - 7/2011
Responsible for a variety of assignments at industrial plant, including:
- *Laboratory Technician*--Tested raw materials for different qualities for specific needs in a laboratory setting, based on accepted industry standards.
- *Machine Operator*—Oversaw the operation of a bank of machines used in the production process and was responsible for all outgoing production of a number of technical production machines.
- *General Forklift*—Basic moving in warehouse environment; knowledge of OSHA standards and safety regulations.
- *Equipment Repair*—Responsible for overseeing all machinery in the production plant and for the repair of any malfunctioning machines, as well as conducting preventative maintenance on machinery.

Labor Ready, Kensington, NJ   4/2008 - 8/2008
Laborer
Temporary employment agency assignments, operating forklift and working on assembly lines in a variety of industrial environments.

Gallatin Recycling, Stanford, PA   3/2006 - 4/2008
Machine Operator
Operated heavy equipment for metal alloy recycling company. Operated bobcat, crane, and excavator. Required knowledge and compliance with OSHA safety standards and licensing.

Pryor Brothers Manufacturing, Cecilia, MA   10/1985 - 3/2006
Production Manager/Machine Operator
- As Production Manager, was responsible for the activities and production of ten employees, including scheduling of work schedules, overseeing quality control of finished work, and ensuring safety of employees and worksite.
- As Machine Operator, operated forklift, excavator, crane, bobcat, and other heavy equipment.

EDUCATION
Darnell High School, Trenton, NJ
GED

SKILLS/EQUIPMENT

Forklift Operation	Bobcat Operation	Crane Operation
Excavator Operation	Supervision	Production Experience
Laboratory Technician	Equipment Repair	Warehouse

Appendix D: Application Tips

A job application may be the employer's first introduction to you. Employers often ask job seekers to fill out an application before they are interviewed. The manner in which you complete your application often tells an employer how well you will perform your job. Since the product you are selling is yourself, it is well worth the time and effort to complete the application to the best of your abilities.

1. Read through the complete application before answering any questions. If handwritten, be sure to print legibly. You should use black or blue ink or pencil, depending on the requirement of the application.

2. Fill in **all** blanks, providing complete, detailed accurate information.

3. Be sure that all names and addresses are spelled correctly. Carry your Social Security card, military discharge papers, special licenses, and other such information with you for reference.

4. Keep a detailed description of your background and work experience with you in order to correctly enter job titles, dates, and company addresses, regardless of how many applications you fill out.

5. A good way to keep this information is to prepare a pocket resume with all pertinent application information which can be carried by you during your job search to help you accurately complete each application.

6. Use appropriate job titles for your previous positions and for positions you are seeking. Have specific jobs in mind.

7. If you are not sure of the wage range for the job you are applying for, write "negotiable" until you have a chance to discuss the job responsibilities with the employer.

8. If you do not have a telephone, ask a friend or neighbor for permission to use their number, and indicate on the application that it is a number where a message may be left.

9. If you have voicemail or an answering machine on the phone you list as your contact number, make sure that the recorded message you have on that machine conveys a professional image. Silly or inappropriate messages—or songs—can hurt your chances to be considered for a job.

10. Ask three people (who are not related to you) if you may use their names for references. Get the current address, occupation and telephone number(s) for each. Some employers ask for business references or names of previous supervisors. You should keep a list of previous supervisors and their contact information. If you have not held a job before, it is permissible to use teachers, pastors, other professionals whom you know, or family friends as references.

11. If there is a special situation in your past, such as a criminal conviction, you should answer specific questions honestly. In this case, it may be best to write "Will explain in interview" in the appropriate blank. This will give the employer a chance to ask relevant questions in a face-to-face interview with you.

12. After you have completed the application, check it over to make sure that the information is thorough

and accurate. If you have any questions about the application or how it should be filled out, ask the person in charge to explain it to you.

13. Usually, you will be asked to sign a statement that the information you have provided is true to the best of your knowledge. False statements made on an application or intentional omissions of information are grounds for termination after being hired.

14. You may be asked to sign a statement giving the employer permission to contact your past employers and check your school and work records. Not signing the statement gives a potential employer the impression that you have something to hide.

15. Always be professional and show respect when filling out an application. Keep in mind that the person who hands you an application may also be involved in the decision to interview and/or hire you. Your behavior and appearance really do matter.

16. If you are asked to complete the application at the job site, it is important to give the impression that you are prepared. Have all your information available, as mentioned in Tip #4. Before leaving home, make sure you have all identification and license information with you.

17. Since some electronic applications are timed, it's important to be well organized and to enter your information as quickly and accurately as possible.

Appendix E: Letter of Explanation
About a Felony Conviction

Name
Address
City, State, Zip Code
Date

Employer Name
Address
City, State, Zip Code

Dear (Prospective Employer):

Please accept this letter of explanation regarding the lack of information on the employment application about my felony conviction of _____ that occurred on _____. I certainly do not want to mislead you or lie to you by not providing more detailed information on the application. However, due to the confidentiality of this information and the embarrassment that I feel over my past mistake(s), I very much want the opportunity to explain this to you in person.

I'm sure you have reservations regarding hiring an ex-offender, and rightfully so. If the positions were reversed, I would probably feel the same way. I can only hope to try to explain the specifics, my true regret for what I have done in the past, why that will never happen again in the future, and—now that I have the opportunity to turn my life around—why I will be an outstanding employee. To back that up, the United States Department of Labor is willing, at no cost to you, to post a $5,000 Fidelity Bond with you on my behalf. Additionally, the Internal Revenue Service offers a one-time $2,400 tax credit to employers who hire ex-offenders.

Whatever your decision may be, I thank you for your time and consideration.

Respectfully,

Name

Appendix F: 100 Sample Interview Questions

Basic Interview Questions:

- Tell me about yourself.

- What are your strengths?

- What are your weaknesses?

- Why do you want this job?

- Where would you like to be in your career five years from now?

- What's your ideal company?

- What attracted you to this company?

- Why should we hire you?

- What did you like least about your last job?

- When were you most satisfied in your job?

- What can you do for us that other candidates can't?

- What were the responsibilities of your last position?

- Why are you leaving your present job?

- What do you know about this industry?

- What do you know about our company?

- Are you willing to relocate?

- Do you have any questions for me?

Behavioral Interview Questions:

- What was the last project you headed up, and what was its outcome?

- Give me an example of a time that you felt you went above and beyond the call of duty at work.

- Can you describe a time when your work was criticized?

- Have you ever been on a team where someone was not pulling their own weight? How did you handle it?

- Tell me about a time when you had to give someone difficult feedback. How did you handle it?

- What is your greatest failure, and what did you learn from it?

- What irritates you about other people, and how do you deal with it?

- If I were your supervisor and asked you to do something that you disagreed with, what would you do?

- What was the most difficult period in your life, and how did you deal with it?

- Tell me about a time where you had to deal with conflict on the job.

- If you were at a business lunch and you ordered a rare steak and they brought it to you well done, what would you do?

- If you found out your company was doing something against the law, like fraud, what would you do?

- What assignment was too difficult for you, and how did you resolve the issue?

- What's the most difficult decision you've made in the last two years and how did you come to that decision?

- Describe how you would handle a situation if you were required to finish multiple tasks by the end of the day, and there was no conceivable way that you could finish them.

Salary Questions:

- What salary are you seeking?

- What's your salary history?

- If I were to give you this salary you requested but let you write your job description for the next year, what would it say?

Career Development Questions:

- What are you looking for in terms of career development?

- How do you want to improve yourself in the next year?

- What kind of goals would you have in mind if you got this job?

- If I were to ask your last supervisor to provide you additional training or exposure, what would she suggest?

Getting Started Questions:

- How would you go about establishing your credibility quickly with the team?

- How long will it take for you to make a significant contribution?

- What do you see yourself doing within the first 30 days of this job?

- If selected for this position, can you describe your strategy for the first 90 days?

More About You:

- How would you describe your work style?

- What would be your ideal working situation?

- What do you look for in terms of culture—structured or entrepreneurial?

- Give examples of ideas you've had or implemented.

- What techniques and tools do you use to keep yourself organized?

- If you had to choose one, would you consider yourself a big-picture person or a detail-oriented person?

- Tell me about your proudest achievement.

- Who was your favorite manager and why?

- What do you think of your previous boss?

- Was there a person in your career who really made a difference?

- What kind of personality do you work best with and why?

- What are you most proud of?

- What do you like to do?

- What are your lifelong dreams?

- What do you ultimately want to become?

- What is your personal mission statement?

- What are three positive things your last boss would say about you?

- What negative thing would your last boss say about you?

- What three character traits would your friends use to describe you?

- What are three positive character traits you don't have?

- If you were interviewing someone for this position, what traits would you look for?

- List five words that describe your character.

- Who has impacted you most in your career and how?

- What is your greatest fear?

- What is your biggest regret and why?

- What's the most important thing you learned in school?

- Why did you choose your major?

- What will you miss about your present/last job?

- What is your greatest achievement outside of work?

- What are the qualities of a good leader? A bad leader?

- Do you think a leader should be feared or liked?

- How do you feel about taking no for an answer?

- How would you feel about working for someone who knows less than you?

- How do you think I rate as an interviewer?

- Tell me one thing about yourself you wouldn't want me to know.

- Tell me the difference between good and exceptional.

- What kind of car do you drive?

- There's no right or wrong answer, but if you could be any where in the world right now, where would you be?

- What's the last book you read?

- What magazines do you subscribe to?

- What's the best movie you've seen in the last year?

- What would you do if you won the lottery?

- Who are your heroes?

- What do you like to do for fun?

- What do you do in your spare time?

- What is your favorite memory from childhood?

Brainteaser Questions:

- How many times do a clock's hands overlap in a day?

- How would you weight a plane without scales?

- Tell me 10 ways to use a pencil other than writing.

- Sell me this pencil.

- If you were an animal, which one would you want to be?

- Why is there fuzz on a tennis ball?

- If you could choose one superhero power, what would it be and why?

- If you could get rid of any one of the U.S. states, which one would you get rid of and why?

- With your eyes closed, tell me step-by-step how to tie my shoes.

Appendix G: Principles of Self-Esteem

1. If you must examine your "faults," do so with a mirror, not a magnifying glass. In other words, don't allow them to assume overwhelming proportions. Instead of "I'll never get out of debt," say "I owe $2,000.00."

2. Learn to do without the word "should." "Shoulds" are often the expectations of others, drilled into our minds at an early age. Substitute "could" for "should." Understand that whenever you do something, you exercise a choice. If you don't like the option you selected this time, you can make a different choice.

3. Graciously accept a compliment. Don't protest. Just say "Thank you."

4. Discard the myth of perfection. Nobody does everything perfectly. We all make mistakes. Just try to learn from them and not repeat them.

5. Endless brooding never solves the problem. Use the problem-solving process to address the problem, then move on.

6. Don't compare yourself with others. Improve yourself.

7. Focus on your strengths, not your weaknesses. Keep a written list of all your accomplishments, however small. Periodically review your list to refresh your memory.

8. Celebrate your accomplishments. Allow yourself to feel good about reaching a goal or accomplishing something.

9. Develop a friendship with someone who really cares about you and who supports you. This should be a person who accepts you for who you are, someone who is trustworthy and with whom you can talk openly and candidly.

10. Count your blessings. Make a list of all the people and things in your life for which you are grateful. Recognize that you are deserving of all these good things.

11. "Do unto others as you would have them do unto you." The Golden Rule never goes out of style. If you're in a position to say "Good morning" to someone or do something nice for someone, do it. You'll see how much others appreciate your efforts and you'll feel better about yourself.

12. We often tend to treat others better than we treat ourselves, so treat yourself the way you would treat another person.

13. Become a more interesting person by being more interested in other people, current events, sports, etc. Become involved in community or church activities.

14. Look at old photographs and reflect on the richness of the events or relationships depicted and how they have enhanced your life.

15. Try to wake in a good frame of mind, which includes a positive attitude and smile. Begin each day with a fun routine. Think about the positive things you can do that day.

16. Put a good picture of yourself in a beautiful frame.

17. Take good care of yourself. Exercise and try to eat healthy foods (low in sugar, salt, and fat content).

18. Periodically do something new or out of the ordinary.

19. Learn a new skill or acquire a new hobby. Find things to do which are interesting and can give you a sense of accomplishment.

20. Go for a walk and enjoy the world around you. Look at the trees, the flowers. Say "hello" to people you pass and make new friends.

21. Take risks. You'll accomplish more and you'll feel good for being brave.

22. Establish some long-term goals. Spend time with yourself to determine where you really want to go and what you really want in the future. Do some in-depth research on how you can realistically reach those goals.

23. Make a "treasure map" of what you want in life. Cut out pictures of the things you really want: a car, a home, a garden, a certain job, the things you want to do—travel, learn to play a musical instrument, play a sport—and of words or images that represent qualities you want more of in your life: love, adventure, sharing, etc. Make a collage of these treasure map pieces and put it where you can see it often.

24. Set small goals that are easy to meet. Allow yourself to feel good about accomplishing these goals.

25. Act confident even if you're not. Eventually, you will feel more confident.

26. Affirm your power to change or to remain the same. Accept that, at this point in time, you may consciously choose a particular behavior as a way to cope, but that you can eventually choose to replace that behavior—for example, a bad habit such as smoking—with a healthier one. This reinforces that **you** control your future and your behavior, and you can shape it in positive rather than negative ways.

Index

ABOUT THE AUTHOR

Cheryl Butler Long is a Workforce Development Specialist with the Division of Workforce Development, Department of Economic Development, for the state of Missouri. She holds professional accreditations as a Global Career Development Facilitator (GCDF), Offender Workforce Development Specialist (OWDS), and Missouri Workforce Development Professional (MWDP). She is also a member of the National Association of Workforce Development Professionals.

She holds a master of liberal arts degree from Baker University, Baldwin City, Kansas, and bachelor of arts degrees in Communication and Public Relations, Magna cum Laude, from William Jewell College, Liberty, Missouri. She graduated from El Segundo High School in El Segundo, California.

The great-granddaughter of James Artherton, occasional member of the Old West Dalton Brothers outlaw gang from Coffeeville, Kansas, she is an accomplished marksman, a member of the USCCA (United States Concealed Carry Association), and an outspoken advocate for Second Amendment rights.

She is also a Notary Public for the state of Missouri. So there!

Job and Career Resources

HE FOLLOWING JOB and career resources are available directly from Impact Publications. Full descriptions of each title – as well as downloadable catalogs, DVDs, software, games, posters, and related products – can be found at www.impactpublications.com. Complete this form or list the titles, include shipping (see the formula on page 151), enclose payment, and send your order to:

IMPACT PUBLICATIONS
9104 Manassas Drive, Suite N
Manassas Park, VA 20111-5211 USA
1-800-361-1055 (orders only)
Tel. 703-361-7300 or Fax 703-335-9486
Email address: query@impactpublications.com
Quick & easy online ordering: www.impactpublications.com

Orders from individuals must be prepaid by check, money order, or major credit card. We accept telephone, fax, and email orders.

Qty.	Titles	Price	TOTAL
Featured Title			
_____	Unemployed, But Moving On!	$13.95	_____
Job Loss and 30/30 Solutions			
_____	Eliminated! Now What?	14.95	_____
_____	Getting Back to Work	15.95	_____
_____	Make Job Loss Work for You	12.95	_____
_____	The Quick 30/30 Job Solution	14.95	_____
_____	Rebound: A Proven Plan for Starting Over After a Job Loss	17.99	_____
_____	Surviving a Layoff: A Week-By-Week Guide to Getting Your Life Back Together	9.99	_____
_____	Surviving a Layoff: Your Guide to a Soft Landing and a Smooth Re-Entry	6.99	_____
Career Exploration and Job Strategies			
_____	10 Laws of Career Reinvention: Essential Survival Skills for Any Economy	15.00	_____
_____	12 Steps to a New Career	16.99	_____
_____	40 Best Fields for Your Career	16.95	_____
_____	50 Best Jobs for Your Personality	17.95	_____
_____	95 Mistakes Job Seekers Make and How to Avoid Them	13.95	_____
_____	100 Fastest Growing Careers	17.95	_____
_____	101 Best Ways to Land a Job in Troubled Times	14.95	_____
_____	150 Best Jobs for a Secure Future	17.95	_____
_____	200 Best Jobs for Renewing America	17.95	_____
_____	200 Best Jobs Through Apprenticeships	24.95	_____
_____	250 Best Paying Jobs	17.95	_____
_____	300 Best Jobs Without a Four-Year Degree	17.95	_____

Qty.	Titles	Price	TOTAL
_____	America's Top Jobs for People Re-Entering the Workforce	19.95	_____
_____	Best Jobs for the 21st Century	19.95	_____
_____	Big Book of Jobs	19.95	_____
_____	Career Mapping	17.95	_____
_____	Change Your Job, Change Your Life	21.95	_____
_____	Cracking the New Job Market	17.95	_____
_____	Directory of Executive and Professional Recruiters	69.95	_____
_____	Get the Career You Want	15.00	_____
_____	Get Hired in a Tough Job Market	16.95	_____
_____	Get the Job You Want, Even When No One's Hiring	19.95	_____
_____	Guerrilla Marketing for Job Hunters 3.0	21.95	_____
_____	Hire Me, Hollywood!	17.95	_____
_____	How to Get a Job and Keep It	16.95	_____
_____	How to Get a Job on Wall Street	16.95	_____
_____	I Found a Job! Career Advice from Job Hunters Who Landed on Their Feet	12.95	_____
_____	Job Hunting Guide: From College to Career	14.95	_____
_____	Job Hunting Tips for People With Hot and Not-So-Hot Backgrounds	17.95	_____
_____	Job Hunter's Survival Guide	9.99	_____
_____	Job Hunting After 50	12.99	_____
_____	Job Search Handbook for People With Disabilities	22.95	_____
_____	Knock 'em Dead	14.95	_____
_____	No One Is Unemployable	29.95	_____
_____	No One Will Hire Me!	15.95	_____
_____	Occupational Outlook Handbook (annual)	19.95	_____
_____	O*NET Dictionary of Occupational Titles	39.95	_____
_____	Overnight Career Choice	9.95	_____
_____	The Quick 30/30 Job Solution	14.95	_____
_____	Quick Job Finding Pocket Guide (packet of 10)	23.60	_____
_____	Quit Your Job and Grow Some Hair	15.95	_____
_____	The Sequel: How to Change Your Career Without Starting Over	12.95	_____
_____	Smart New Way to Get Hired	14.95	_____
_____	Strategies for Successful Career Change	16.99	_____
_____	Top 100 Careers Without a Four-Year Degree	18.95	_____
_____	Top 300 Careers	18.95	_____
_____	What Color Is Your Parachute?	18.99	_____

Internet Job Search

Qty.	Titles	Price	TOTAL
_____	America's Top Internet Job Sites	19.95	_____
_____	Best Career and Education Websites	14.95	_____
_____	Directory of Websites for International Jobs	19.95	_____
_____	Guide to Internet Job Searching	16.95	_____
_____	Job Nation: The 100 Best Employment Sites on the Web	14.95	_____
_____	Job Seeker's Online Goldmine	13.95	_____
_____	What Color Is Your Parachute? Guide to Job-Hunting Online	12.99	_____

Qty.	Titles	Price	TOTAL
Interviews			
_____	101 Dynamite Questions to Ask At Your Job Interview	13.95	_____
_____	101 Great Answers to the Toughest Interview Questions	12.99	_____
_____	301 Best Questions to Ask On Your Interview	14.95	_____
_____	301 Smart Answers to Tough Interview Questions	12.95	_____
_____	Best Answers to 201 Most Frequently Asked Interview Questions	14.95	_____
_____	Can I Wear My Nose Ring to the Interview?	13.95	_____
_____	Everything Practice Interview Book	14.95	_____
_____	I Can't Believe They Asked Me That!	17.95	_____
_____	Instant Interviews	16.95	_____
_____	Interview Magic	18.95	_____
_____	Job Interview Tips for People With Not-So-Hot Backgrounds	14.95	_____
_____	Job Interview Phrase Book	10.95	_____
_____	Job Interviews for Dummies	16.99	_____
_____	KeyWords to Nail the Job Interview	17.95	_____
_____	Nail the Job Interview!	14.95	_____
_____	The Savvy Interviewer	10.95	_____
_____	Tell Me About Yourself	14.95	_____
_____	Win the Interview, Win the Job	15.95	_____
_____	Winning Job Interviews	12.99	_____
_____	You Have 3 Minutes!	21.95	_____
_____	You Should Hire Me!	15.95	_____
Social Media			
_____	Find a Job Through Social Networking	14.95	_____
_____	How to Find a Job on LindedIn, Facebook, Twitter, MySpace,and Other Social Networks	18.95	_____
_____	Twitter Job Search Guide	14.95	_____
_____	Web 2.0 Job Finder	15.99	_____
Salary Negotiations			
_____	101 Salary Secrets	12.95	_____
_____	250 Best-Paying Jobs	16.95	_____
_____	Get a Raise in 7 Days	14.95	_____
_____	Give Me More Money!	17.95	_____
_____	Salary Negotiation Tips for Professionals	16.95	_____
_____	Salary Tutor	13.99	_____
_____	Secrets of Power Salary Negotiating	13.99	_____
Attitude and Motivation			
_____	100 Ways to Motivate Yourself	14.99	_____
_____	Attitude Is Everything	16.99	_____
_____	Change Your Thinking, Change Your Life	19.95	_____
_____	Goals!	15.95	_____
_____	Little Gold Book of YES! Attitude	19.99	_____
_____	Success Principles	17.95	_____

Qty.	Titles	Price	TOTAL

Inspiration and Empowerment

_____	7 Habits of Highly Effective People	15.95	_____
_____	101 Secrets of Highly Effective Speakers	15.95	_____
_____	Create Your Own Future	19.95	_____
_____	Life Strategies	13.95	_____
_____	The Magic of Thinking Big	14.00	_____
_____	The Power of Positive Thinking	14.95	_____
_____	Power of Purpose	17.95	_____
_____	Practical Wisdom	26.95	_____
_____	We Have Met the Enemy	26.95	_____
_____	Who Moved My Cheese?	19.95	_____

Testing and Assessment

_____	Career, Aptitude, and Selections Tests	17.95	_____
_____	Career Match	15.00	_____
_____	Discover What You're Best At	14.95	_____
_____	Do What You Are	18.99	_____
_____	Employment Personality Tests Decoded	16.99	_____
_____	The Everything Career Tests Book	12.95	_____
_____	I Want to Do Something Else,But I'm Not Sure		
	What It Is	15.95	_____
_____	Now, Discover Your Strengths	30.00	_____
_____	What Should I Do With My Life?	16.00	_____
_____	What Type Am I?	16.00	_____
_____	What's Your Type of Career?	21.95	_____

Resumes and Letters

_____	101 Great Tips for a Dynamite Resume	13.95	_____
_____	201 Dynamite Job Search Letters	19.95	_____
_____	Best KeyWords for Resumes, Cover Letters, & Interviews	17.95	_____
_____	Best Resumes and CVs for International Jobs	24.95	_____
_____	Best Resumes for $100,000+ Jobs	24.95	_____
_____	Best Resumes for People Without a Four-Year Degree	19.95	_____
_____	Blue-Collar Resume and Job Hunting Guide	15.95	_____
_____	Competency-Based Resumes	13.99	_____
_____	Cover Letter Magic	18.95	_____
_____	Cover Letters for Dummies	16.99	_____
_____	Cover Letters That Knock'em Dead	12.95	_____
_____	Create Your Digital Portfolio	26.95	_____
_____	Expert Resumes for Career Changers	16.95	_____
_____	Expert Resumes for Computer and Web Jobs	17.95	_____
_____	Expert Resumes for Health Care Careers	16.95	_____
_____	Expert Resumes for People Returning to Work	16.95	_____
_____	Haldane's Best Cover Letters for Professionals	15.95	_____
_____	Haldane's Best Resumes for Professionals	15.95	_____
_____	High Impact Resumes and Letters	19.95	_____
_____	Military-to-Civilian Resumes and Letters	21.95	_____
_____	Nail the Cover Letter!	17.95	_____

Qty.	Titles	Price	TOTAL
_____	Nail the Resume!	17.95	_____
_____	Resume, Application, and Letter Tips for		
	People With Hot and Not-So-Hot Backgrounds	17.95	_____
_____	Resumes for Dummies	16.99	_____
_____	Resumes That Knock 'Em Dead	12.95	_____
_____	The Savvy Resume Writer	12.95	_____
_____	Step-By-Step Resumes	19.95	_____
_____	Winning Letters That Overcome Barriers to Employment	17.95	_____

Networking

Qty.	Titles	Price	TOTAL
_____	Fine Art of Small Talk	16.95	_____
_____	Little Black Book of Connections	19.95	_____
_____	Masters of Networking	18.95	_____
_____	Networking for People Who Hate Networking	18.95	_____
_____	Never Eat Alone	26.00	_____
_____	One Phone Call Away	22.95	_____
_____	Power Networking	14.95	_____
_____	The Savvy Networker	13.95	_____
_____	Work the Pond!	16.95	_____

Dress, Image, and Etiquette

Qty.	Titles	Price	TOTAL
_____	Business Etiquette for Dummies	21.99	_____
_____	Dressing Smart for Men	16.95	_____
_____	Dressing Smart for the New Millennium	15.95	_____
_____	Dressing Smart for Women	16.95	_____
_____	Power Etiquette	15.95	_____
_____	You've Only Got Three Seconds	15.00	_____

Military in Transition

Qty.	Titles	Price	TOTAL
_____	Expert Resumes for Military-to-Civilian Transition	16.95	_____
_____	Military-to-Civilian Resumes and Letters	21.95	_____
_____	Military-to-Civilian Career Transition Guide	14.95	_____
_____	Military-to-Civilian Transition Guide	13.95	_____
_____	Military to Federal Career Guide	18.95	_____
_____	Military Spouse's Complete Guide to Career Success	17.95	_____
_____	Military Transition to Civilian Success	21.95	_____

Ex-Offenders and Re-Entry Success

Qty.	Titles	Price	TOTAL
_____	Best Jobs for Ex-Offenders	9.95	_____
_____	Best Resumes and Letters for Ex-Offenders	19.95	_____
_____	Ex-Offender's 30/30 Job Solution	9.95	_____
_____	Ex-Offender's Job Hunting Guide	17.95	_____
_____	Ex-Offender's Job Interview Guide	9.95	_____
_____	Ex-Offender's Quick Job Hunting Guide	9.95	_____
_____	Ex-Offender's Re-Entry Success Guide	9.95	_____
_____	Putting the Bars Behind You Survival Guides	69.95	_____

Qty.	Titles	Price	TOTAL
Government and Security Jobs			
_____	Book of U.S. Government Jobs	27.95	_____
_____	Complete Guide to Public Employment	19.95	_____
_____	FBI Careers	19.95	_____
_____	Post Office Jobs	24.95	_____
_____	Ten Steps to a Federal Job	28.95	_____
International and Travel Jobs			
_____	Back Door Guide to Short-Term Job Adventures	21.95	_____
_____	Careers in International Affairs	24.95	_____
_____	Jobs for Travel Lovers	19.95	_____
_____	Teaching English Abroad	24.95	_____

SUBTOTAL _____
Virginia residents add 5% sales tax

POSTAGE/HANDLING $5.00 +
($5 for first product and 9% of SUBTOTAL)   additional:

9% of SUBTOTAL
(Include an additional 15% if shipping
outside the continental United States)   _____

TOTAL ENCLOSED   _____

SHIP TO:

Name: _____

Address: _____

_____

_____

PAYMENT METHOD:

☐ I enclose check/money order for $ _____ made payable to
IMPACT PUBLICATIONS.

☐ Please charge $ _____ to my credit card:

☐ Visa   ☐ MasterCard   ☐ American Express   ☐ Discover

Card # _____Expiration date: ____ / ____

Signature _____

Employment & Re-Entry
Solutions for Today's Economy!

Resources that literally put you to work!

Unemployed, But Moving On!
Smart Job Searching in a Web-Based World and a Sucky Economy
Cheryl Butler Long

New!

A hard-hitting and compelling must-read for anyone trying to get a job in a struggling economy. The author challenges common assumptions and tells it like it really is from the perspective of a street-smart employment expert who works daily with the unemployed and those with not-so-hot backgrounds. Covers everything from writing resumes and letters, completing applications, and networking to conducting interviews, starting the job, and getting fired. Includes special chapters on ex-offenders and people facing discrimination in the job market. October 2011. 160 pages. ISBN 978-1-57023-325-8. **$13.95**

The Quick 30/30 Job Solution:
Smart Job Search Tips for Surviving Today's New Economy
Neil P. McNulty and Ronald L. Krannich, Ph.D.

Introduces the concept of the 30/30 Job Search™, which has been successfully used by thousands of clients. Outlines a powerful 30-day program for finding job opportunities within 30 miles of any community. Reveals an arsenal of unconventional strategies and techniques that get the attention of prospective employers, from using voicemail to scheduling interviews and following up. Here's the book that can make a big difference in the life of anyone who needs to quickly find a job in today's economy. 2010. 176 pages. ISBN 978-1-57023-286-2. **$14.95**

Job Hunting Tips for People With Hot and Not-So-Hot Backgrounds (2nd Edition)
Ronald L. Krannich, Ph.D.

Individual chapters include revealing tips on assessing skills and abilities, developing an objective, completing applications, networking, writing resumes and letters, following up, interviewing for jobs, and negotiating salaries and terms of employment. Filled with cutting-edge career advice, quizzes, websites, and examples. 2010. 240 pages. ISBN 978-1-57023-307-4. **$17.95**

Military-to-Civilian Transition Guide
15th Edition
Carl S. Savino and Ronald L. Krannich, Ph.D.

With more than 3.5 million copies in print, this remains the most popular career transition guide for servicemembers, veterans, and their families – "The Gold Standard" for making a successful career transition. Covers everything from organizing an effective job search, obtaining transition assistance, developing employer-centered objectives to writing resumes, networking, interviewing, and finding a government job. ISBN 978-0-9838489-0-5. 160 pages. 2012. **$13.95**

The Ex-Offender's Quick Job Hunting Guide
Bestseller!
Ronald L. Krannich, Ph.D.

Packed with practical insights, self-tests, and exercises, this book is designed to implement 10 key steps for re-entering the work world. Includes special sections on changing attitudes, community assistance, networking, completing applications, writing resumes, handling rejections, interviewing, taking responsibility, telling the truth, and developing an action plan. 128 pages. 2009. ISBN 978-1-57023-285-5. **$9.95**

Job Search Solutions for Tough Times
The A to Z's of Overcoming Barriers to Employment
Bestsellers!
Ron and Caryl Krannich, Ph.Ds

Five bestselling guides by two of America's leading career experts help job seekers develop an effective job search that quickly overcomes barriers to employment. Addresses the A to Z's of setting goals, writing resumes, networking, interviewing, negotiating salary, starting fresh, and more. Can purchase separately. **SPECIAL: $79.95 for complete set of five books.**

- No One Will Hire Me! ($15.95)
- Overcoming Barriers to Employment ($17.95)
- Resume, Application, and Letter Tips for People With Hot and Not-So-Hot Backgrounds ($17.95)
- Win the Interview, Win the Job ($15.95)
- You Should Hire Me! ($15.95)

Quantity discounts on all books featured on this page

Number Copies	% Discount	Number Copies	% Discount
10-24	20%	1,000-4,999	60%
25-49	30%	5,000-24,999	65%
50-99	40%	25,000-49,999	70%
100-499	50%	50,000-99,999	75%
500-999	55%	100,000+ copies	80%

SPECIAL: Purchase all 10 books on this page for $139.95 – Employment and Re-Entry Solutions (set of 10)